The Grandparents' Handbook

A Practical Guide to Enjoying
the New Generation

Introduced by Dr. Hugh Jolly

Managing Editor   Susan Pinkus
Production Manager   David Alexander
Photographic Coordinator   Siân Phillips
Administration   Aline Davis, Sonia White
Design   Behram Kapadia

Recipes and all accompanying illustrations were provided by The Butter Information Council, The Flour Advisory Bureau, The National Dairy Council, The Potato Marketing Board, Cadbury Schweppes, The Apple and Pear Development Council, Findus, The British Sugar Bureau, Mattessons, and The Eggs Information Bureau.

Illustrations by Design Practitioners Limited and Temple Art Agency

Photography by Anthea Sieveking

The Publishers gratefully acknowledge the cooperation of all those individuals and organizations who have contributed to **The Grandparents' Handbook,** in particular K.C. Fulton, MD, MRCS, LRCP; Beryl Downing; Grosvenor Books (for the extract on page 19) The Royal Society for the Prevention of Accidents; and Robson Rhodes, Chartered Accountants.

© 1984 Pagoda Books, London

All rights reserved. No part of this publication may be reproduced, stored in a retrieval system or transmitted in any form or by any means, electronic, mechanical, photocopying, recording or otherwise, without the prior permission of the publishers.

Publishers' Note

Although our aim has been to provide a general guide from a grandparent's point of view to infant and child care, the advice contained in **The Grandparents' Handbook** cannot embrace all circumstances, nor is it intended as a substitute for consultation with a doctor. Serious problems will, of course, require expert and sometimes prompt medical care.

ISBN: 0-86683-847-3
Library of Congress Catalog Card Number: 84 : 50003
Origination by East Anglian Engraving
Typeset by Di-alogue
Printed in Great Britain by Blantyre Printing and Binding Ltd.

The Grandparents' Handbook

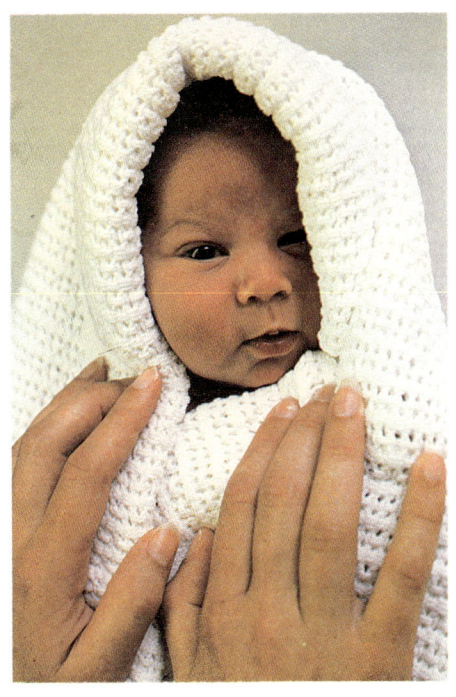

This book is dedicated
by the publishers to
all grandparents, everywhere

Contents

	Pages
Foreword	5
A new role	7 - 19
Guess who's coming to stay!	20 - 25
Safety steps	26 - 27
Safety at home	28 - 29
Traveling with children	30 - 33
Children and pets	34 - 35
Outings and treats	36 - 37
Fun in the yard	38 - 41
Things to make	42 - 51
Bon appetit!	52 - 59
Games galore	60 - 65
Choosing toys	66 - 71
First aid	72 - 73
Grandma, I don't feel well!	74 - 75
Coping with problems	76 - 81
A helping hand	82 - 83
Family photographs	84 - 87
The family tree	88 - 91
Memorandum	92 - 95
Further reading	96
Index	96

Foreword

The chances are that for most new grandparents, it has been some twenty years at least since they last handled a baby, looked after a toddler, or played regularly with a small child. That's why **The Grandparents' Handbook** was conceived, not only to provide an invaluable revision course in infant care, but also to offer suggestions as to games, meals, outings, and treats to be enjoyed with the new generation. For the grandparent does indeed have an all-important role to play within the family circle.

Dr. Hugh Jolly, the eminent British pediatrician, whose books on child care have guided so many parents over the years, has contributed a major section to **The Grandparents' Handbook.** In it, he explores the nature of the grandparent – grandchild relationship, explains various new developments in child care theory (while debunking some old wives' tales), and takes the reader through the basic principles of such everyday essentials as feeding, carrying, bathing, and changing.

Other sections are devoted to a wise choice of toys for the growing child, how best to look after your grandchild when he is sick, making a family tree, and first aid and safety in the home. Learn something, too, from *The Grandparent Game* on pages 78–79. This has been designed as an instructive entertainment in its own right. You are bound to make a few mistakes in the 'game'; most grandparents will. What is important is to benefit from experience, to foresee potential problem areas, and to learn how to cope with family frictions, should they arise.

Throughout **The Grandparents' Handbook,** you will find that our contributors refer in the main to the grandchild as 'he'. This, the publishers would like to emphasize, has merely been chosen as a convenient pronoun.

Congratulations on becoming a grandparent! It is a natural role but one that inevitably requires some working at. The publishers hope that grandmothers and grandfathers will find many useful hints on the pages that follow.

A new role

"Seven pounds, four ounces. Mother and baby both doing well." Perhaps it's your first grandchild, or maybe you are already an old hand. No matter. The news will still be just as thrilling, and if you enjoyed the growing years with your own young family, you will almost certainly enjoy the time ahead even more. For the grandparent's role is a special one and you have a very personal contribution to make to your grandchild's growth and development. The chances are you need him or her, too, for the desire to have grandchildren can be very strong.

Surveys show that the average age of a new grandparent in the western hemisphere is around forty-seven; but of course a great many are older, and many even younger. Some grandparents find they subsequently bear children who will be younger than their grandchildren, but that is rare. The very word 'grandparent' traditionally conjures up either a white-haired old lady, sporting spectacles and an apron, or an elderly, bald man, with a pipe in his mouth. Yet most new grandparents are in the prime of life, still working and probably physically very fit. So becoming a grandparent should not make you feel old, as some new grandparents have been heard to complain.

Instead, contact with the new generation should prove both invigorating and rejuvenating. Many grandparents even say that they far prefer grandparenting to parenting. You will certainly find that it alters your relationship with your own children, probably bringing you all far closer together. Parents-in-law rock the boat, it is sometimes said; grandparents rock the cradle.

Most of us undoubtedly look forward to having grandchildren. But why? In 1964, two researchers, Neugarten and Weinstein, completed a major investigation into the psychology of grandparenting. Many people, they found, expressed a desire for biological renewal, for a continuing of the family line. Others wished for emotional self-fulfillment which they felt could be achieved as a result of companionship and good times with their grandchildren. Some thought they would enjoy providing the resources of experience, as well as financial aid and time. Others wanted to see the achievement by their grandchildren of things they had no chance themselves to achieve.

Neugarten and Weinstein went on to classify grandparents into various types. The *formal*, they said, were interested in their grandchildren, would provide special treats, and would babysit but left actual parenting to the parents, not interfering or offering advice. The *fun-seekers* were informal, saw grandparenting as a leisure activity, and expected a mutually satisfying, playful relationship with their grandchildren. The *surrogates* assumed responsibilities when the mother was working. Those referred to as *reservoirs of wisdom* were distinctly authoritarian, regarding both their children and grandchildren as subordinates, and dispensing special skills or resources. The *distant figures*, meanwhile, were often benevolent but had infrequent and fleeting contact. The results of these studies are reported in detail in the *Journal of Marriage and the Family, 1964* (26,199-204) in a feature entitled *The Changing American Grandparent*.

In 1977, another American study looked specifically at different styles of grandmothering. Researcher J.F. Robertson found that twenty-six percent of those interviewed could be labeled *symbolic*: that is, their main focus was on what is morally right and on setting a good example. Another group, labeled *individualized*, were more concerned with deriving emotional satisfaction from their grandchildren than with their upbringing. The third group (about twenty-nine percent) were labeled *apportioned* and were concerned both with what is right for a child *and* with emotional satisfaction. Approximately one-third were described as remote, uninvolved or unconcerned with their role. There were distinct differences; yet as many as eighty percent agreed that a good grandparent is one who loves and enjoys grandparenthood, who sets a good example, provides help, is a good listener but does not interfere. The results of this study, too, are reported in the *Journal of Marriage and the Family, 1977* (39,165-174) in an article headed *Grandmotherhood: a study of role conceptions*.

A matter of heredity

Even before you become a grandparent officially, and even prior to your grandchild's conception, there are ways in which you can contribute to producing a healthy, bouncing member of the next generation. For heredity is not just a matter of brown skin, blue eyes, or red hair. There may be far more important things at stake; and it is undoubtedly a grandparent's specific duty to tell the family about any conditions that are known to be hereditary: for example, *diabetes, sickle-cell*

A new role

anemia (prevalent among the black population), high blood pressure, *hemophilia, muscular dystrophy,* and certain abnormal biochemical conditions. Sometimes such inherited diseases may skip a generation or affect only one sex but be carried by the other, as with *hemophilia*, in which there is failure of the clotting mechanism of the blood. Genetic counseling can be very helpful in reducing the risk of recurrence of such conditions.

Tay-Sachs disease, for instance, is found almost exclusively among the Jewish population of Eastern European origin, and the children who suffer from it literally waste away, usually some time before the fourth birthday. Both parents must be carriers for the one-in-four chance to occur, and a simple blood test will indicate if the prospective parents are carriers. That is why members of this Jewish community are encouraged to have the test prior to considering marriage and child-bearing. Similarly, a blood disease known as *thalassemia,* in which the body's red blood cells do not last the normal ninety days, resulting in severe anemia, is also inherited as a recessive trait. Until recently, it was particularly common among the Greek Cypriot population: but, as a result of a campaign of genetic counseling (both parents must be carriers for there to be a risk of the child inheriting the disease), the incidence was almost wiped out in Cyprus in 1983.

A parent who has a *dominant* abnormal gene will be suffering from the condition in question; and even if the other parent has no such abnormality, half the next generation may be affected. A *recessively* inherited disorder, however, results from both parents being carriers, and the proportionate odds are that one in four of their children may actually suffer from the disease, with two being healthy carriers like themselves and one being normal. *Cystic fibrosis* is another example of this. Of course, the chances of someone carrying the same abnormal gene as a marriage partner are small; but this risk is increased when members of the same family – cousins, for instance – marry, which is why this is medically discouraged. Some peoples, however, actually encourage marriage among relatives since, by tradition, they wish to retain wealth within the family. But whatever the pattern of affected children, no guarantee that the next child will be normal can ever be made. The chance that a coin will fall heads or tails is equal on every occasion.

Take comfort in the fact, however, that only a very small proportion of babies are born with even a minor abnormality. The chances are good that your grandchild will be a healthy infant in every respect.

New theories for old

If statistics are anything to go by, it has probably been some twenty years since you last had regular contact with a small baby. In that time, there have been so many changes in child care theory that you may at first feel confused. But is bringing up an infant today really so different? Were all the things you did for *your* children actually so undesirable.

Doubts may be manifold, but a common sense approach to new developments is all that is required for a clear understanding of the why's and wherefore's. What may surprise the grandparent most of all, and particularly the prospective *grandfather*, is the extent to which fathers now take an active interest in preparation for labor and are present at the birth. This is virtually routine today in some countries, except where a parent specifically expresses a wish to the contrary, or where there are complications. The

The prospect of picking up a tiny infant is always a little worrying at first, but babies are more hardy than they look. Use one hand to support your grandchild's head and the other to support his lower half when lifting him. Then either cradle him, supporting his head in the crook of your arm, or hold him against the upper part of your chest with his head on your shoulder, as shown in the illustrations here.

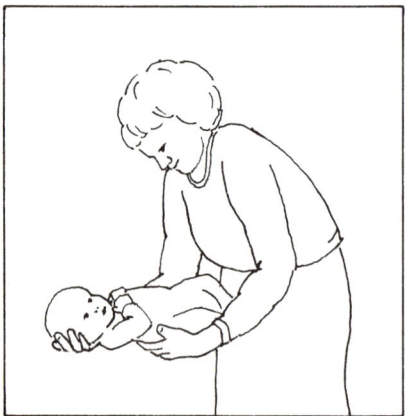
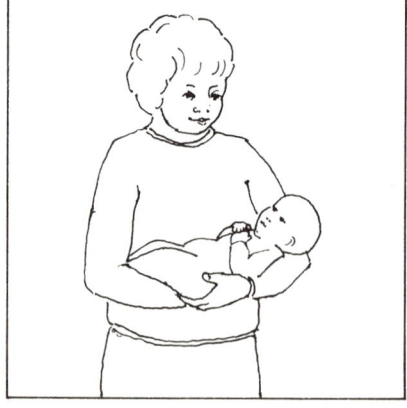

father, after all, has been pregnant too for a period of nine months, if psychologically rather than physically; and his intimate involvement and assistance with labor can be of the greatest help. Many companies now also grant paternity leave in recognition of the importance of the new father's role.

You may find, too, that your daughter or daughter-in-law opts for what is now known as 'natural childbirth'; that is, childbirth with minimum medical intervention and without use of pain-relieving drugs unless absolutely necessary, following a pre-natal course of breathing and exercise techniques to ease labor. Progressive hospitals encourage a mother to choose the position that she finds most comfortable for childbirth, particularly squatting. Taking part in the birth in this active manner is far more beneficial for both parents and baby, as long as they agree that the obstetrician or midwife take over should circumstances demand it.

You will find, too, that during the last few years there has been a tremendous change in the emphasis placed on the importance of breastfeeding. Breast is best, the experts now agree; and most mothers are able to breastfeed if skilled encouragement is given. The value of breastfeeding can be summarized as follows. Breast milk is the perfect food for the baby, is always readily available at the right temperature, and it is less likely to produce an overweight infant. The first milk produced by the breasts – *colostrum* – helps give a baby greater resistance to infection. A breastfed baby will have closer physical contact with his mother, there should be no risk of milk allergy, and he will not become constipated while breastfed; so that, all in all, it is most definitely advisable for a mother to breastfeed her baby. Do everything you can to support your daughter or daughter-in-law in her decision. It is also, of course, *free*.

All this is not to say that the mother who opts to bottle-feed, in spite of the advantages of breastfeeding, should be made to feel guilty. A modern formula will provide quite adequate nourishment for a growing baby, and he or she can be cradled when bottle-fed so that all-important physical contact is maintained. But current medical thinking is definitely pro-breast, and 'demand-feeding' (feeding when the baby literally 'asks' to be fed by his cries) is preferable to following the clock. The low protein content of human milk actually means that an infant will require frequent and almost continuous feeding in the early days. Weaning is not widely recommended until about six months; but the best approach is a flexible one. Rules, remember, are no more than convenient guidelines, at least as far as babies are concerned. Many old rules were based on an inadquate knowledge of physiology.

Ordinary cows' milk is now known to be unsuitable for a newborn baby, as its sodium content is too high. A commercially made formula is, however, quite suitable and should be used for the first six months if a baby is bottle-fed.

Views on circumcision, too, once widely advocated for health reasons, now vary. In the U.K., it is now out of style and no longer considered necessary other than in exceptional circumstances – for example, when the foreskin is forced back before it becomes separate naturally. Religious custom requiring circumcision in the Jewish and Moslem communities, meanwhile, persists. Most U.K. doctors are not at all eager to operate without a very good medical reason, as they consider there is always a certain element of risk. In the U.S., however, circumcision is widely practiced, though becoming less frequent.

Childrearing practices tend to vary not only from generation to generation but also from family to family, and this is particularly true of the use of pacifiers. In my view, a baby is far better off sucking his thumb than a pacifier, if additional sucking comfort is required. It will enable the baby to explore both his mouth and other objects, which he cannot possibly do with a pacifier. A pacifier also acts as a plug, blocking the baby's attempts at early sounds. If someone *has* given your grandchild a pacifier, do be sure never to dip it into honey or some other sweet substance that may cause dental decay. Whenever you are tempted to use a pacifier to stop a baby crying, remember that a cuddle is usually far more comforting and thus more effective.

The new mother

The arrival of a first baby will almost certainly alter to a great extent the new parents' way of life. It is even sometimes said that their relationship will never be the same again, although this does not necessarily mean that things will deteriorate. In fact, the birth of a baby will usually bring everyone far closer together. It is, however, a time of mutual readjustment, calling for great sensitivity on everyone's part.

At first, it is only natural that a great deal of attention will be given to the new arrival. The mother, too, may be virtually hypnotized by her infant. But the mother also requires attention if her well-being (both physical and emotional) is to be maintained after the birth, and the baby's healthy development will in turn depend on his mother's post-natal progress. So all the help you can give your daughter or daughter-in-law soon after the birth will probably be welcomed with open arms. This will be particularly true if the birth has been strenuous, if there was a caesarian

A new role

section, or if time is needed to recover from an episiotomy (that is, a cut to facilitate delivery) or from the effect of pain-relieving drugs given during labor, for example. Her diet following the birth will be of the utmost importance. Perhaps you could assist here, too, either by helping with the shopping or by preparing some well-balanced meals for the freezer. It will always also be preferable if you can visit to look after an older grandchild at such a time rather than changing his environment.

You will be sensible, too, to ensure that the new mother is not overtired by too many visitors, however well-meaning they are. Short visits will be preferable, and appreciated, to begin with, and this will be particularly true while the new mother is in the hospital. Watch for signs of the 'baby blues'. A number of mothers feel a little depressed soon after the birth, perhaps as a result of their emotional state, perhaps because of nervousness, or perhaps as a reaction to the birth as an anti-climax. Even normally very confident women are sometimes affected in this way. It takes time to fall in love with your baby just as it does with a spouse. The new baby may not look that beautiful at first, or he or she may be the 'wrong' sex. Usually these feelings are transient and soon pass, especially if family and the hospital staff are sensitive and understanding. Severe post-natal depression is rare and is, I believe, preventable if problems are discussed openly both pre-natally and post-natally. Don't be tempted to tell the new mother to snap out of it. It may take a little time for her to become herself again.

Encourage the new mother to attend post-natal exercise classes and to keep her post-natal medical appointments. She may appreciate your company for these. Help her establish something of a routine, and lend all the emotional support you can, for the new mother may find herself having to cope with something of a revolution in her life, particularly if she has been very independent in her own right and working until not long before the birth. New parents often value a little time to themselves; that is only natural. So you may like to offer to stay with the baby while his parents go for a refreshing walk or even an evening out. Babies have needs, and so do parents!

If you visit the hospital soon after your grandchilds' birth, you may be surprised to find him in a crib next to his mother's bed, as is the practice in many hospitals. Some also encourage a mother to keep her baby in bed with her. There is no risk of smothering the baby unless the mother has taken a sedative or is under the influence of alcohol: and having her baby in bed with her at first can greatly increase the intensity of the mother-baby relationship. (It would probably not be wise, however, for a grandparent to adopt such a procedure since the natural maternal instincts that prevent you from accidentally rolling over on the baby may be less intense.)

Attitudes toward colic, burping and gas have also changed. There is in fact no evidence at all to show that babies are any more likely to be full of air than are adults. An X-ray would show the abdominal cavity in most people to be half fluid, half air. *Colic* – a term used to describe abdominal pain as a result of the intestine undergoing contraction because of an obstruction – was once widely ascribed to excessive gas. The colicky, crying baby was thought to draw his legs up in pain, but in fact all babies do this instinctively, when crying for whatever reason, if there is no blanket over them to restrict movement. The baby who cries incessantly in this way, however, if he is otherwise healthy and well-fed, could be revealing through his crying some other, possibly deep-seated problem in the mother-infant relationship. I have even seen a very tense mother cause her baby to scream merely by her presence, almost as if reacting to an electric shock. Babies can be very accurate barometers of their mothers' feelings.

It is now considered unwise to put continual crying down to gas, when it may have other, perhaps emotional causes. Some countries, Czechoslovakia for one, do not even practice what they see as the strange English and American habit of burping the baby. The basic rule must always be to pick up a crying baby unless, of course, you are so tense for some reason that this in itself could be counterproductive.

Only in the years since you had your own family have the dangers of smoking been brought to light: and most pediatricians now agree that it is grossly unfair to subject an infant or child to it. Surveys show a higher incidence of respiratory infections in children if there is smoking in the house. If you smoke, try not to do so in your grandchild's presence. This applies to pipes and cigars as well as to cigarettes.

Nursery needs

Traditionally, grandparents like to buy some part of the new baby's layette or an item for the nursery, and there is undoubtedly great pleasure to be had from a shopping expedition of this kind.

Some grandparents will be on very limited budgets, but they can still contribute a gift of some kind, if only because not everything for the baby needs to be new. Hunt through those old suitcases or chests and see what you have packed away. It could be that for sentimental reasons you have kept some of your own children's baby clothes – a christening robe or shawl, perhaps. How wonderful to be able to hand down such an

A new role

Make sure you are comfortable when feeding and that the bottle is tilted so that the nipple is always full of milk.

Remember to find out about any particular likes and dislikes if you are cooking for your grandchild.

heirloom! Small baby items are also very quick and inexpensive to knit or sew, but don't overdo things. Babies grow very quickly, and it will not be necessary to have a whole wardrobe of beautiful items in the very smallest size. Other relatives and friends are also likely to give the baby gifts of some kind, so it may be sensible to make just a few really exquisite items. Get color-wise, too. For some incomprehensible reason, baby clothes usually come in pale pink, pale blue, or white. Why not choose brighter shades? Babies can look marvelous in red, bottle green, navy blue, or yellow. There is an added bonus in that garments will not look quite so grubby quite so quickly.

It may be advisable to check with the parents, and the other set of grandparents, if you plan to purchase a major nursery item, just to ensure that something similar has not already been acquired. Here again, not everything needs to be new. The local want ads may yield a good find in almost perfect condition. Check that the item is still quite safe and stable, and that nontoxic paint has been used. You may even choose to hunt for a fine antique – a low nursing chair, for example, or an old chest of drawers, an old rocking horse, or a decorative crib.

The following items would almost certainly be welcomed by new parents, and also find a useful place in the nursery.

Clothing

Look for soft nonflammable materials and garments that open in front so that there is no need to turn the baby over when changing him. Requirements will vary according to season and climate, but a fairly basic wardrobe would include the baby garments listed below, any combinations of which would make an excellent gift:
- 3 or 4 stretch suits that undo easily to facilitate diaper changing
- 3 or 4 undershirts with ample openings at the neck
- 2 or 3 gowns or kimonos
- 2 pairs of mittens and bootees (avoid those made with nylon thread as this can cut off the blood supply if it comes loose and gets wrapped around a baby's finger)
- 3 or 4 small baby blankets
- 2 bonnets
- 2 jackets or sweaters
- 1 baby's sleeping bag or outerwear (this should not be slippery)
- christening robe
- shawl
- plastic pants

Note: no shoes are necessary until the baby is walking. It will be far better if his feet are allowed maximum freedom.

11

A new role

Nursery furniture
- chest of drawers
- cupboard or shelving units
- changing table or mat
- comfortable nursing chair
- soft toys
- safety mattress
- cot mirror
- safety gate
- cradle, crib, lined basket, or portable crib (a full-size bed will not be necessary for some time). There should be no rough surfaces, and the bars on the crib should be vertical and close together so that the baby cannot get his head stuck between them
- high chair
- baby walker
- baby bouncer
- playpen
- for the crib: sheets, blankets (satin-edged, not fringed), cotton or flannel crib pads, and *no* pillows (there is danger of suffocation)
- baby intercom alarm
- dimmer-switch
- mobile
- toy box

For a journey
- fabric-sided portable crib
- buggy or stroller (if buying secondhand, check the brakes and see that all safety standards are met)
- backpack or sling for carrying the baby
- diaper bag
- baby seat for a car
- set of reins, for once the baby is walking
- holdall for baby equipment

For feeding
- bibs
- hand food grinder
- steamer
- sterilizing equipment and bottle-warmer (necessary only for bottle-feeding)
- blender (or juicer)
- nonbreakable, decorative baby plates
- silver spoon set
- nonspill drinking mugs

For the bathroom
- baby soap, oils, and lotions
- 2-3 dozen cloth diapers or a large supply of disposable diapers
- soft towels
- hair brush
- baby bath tub
- nonslip bath mat
- bath toys

A basic revision course

Since the chances are that it is some time since you last had close contact with a small baby, the guidelines that follow are provided as a basic summary of certain all-important points relevant to feeding, bathing, carrying and generally caring for the new infant. After many years, it may take a while for your confidence in all these areas to resurface, but rest assured that, within a very short time and with just a little practice, you will become expert again.

Babies may look delicate, but they are really much more hardy than you probably imagine. A newborn has no control over his head, however, so when you pick him up, you need to do so in a way that will support the head. Hold the baby fairly firmly; this will ensure a sense of security. If you walk around with the baby, do so gently and with an even step. Either cradle the baby in the crook of an arm, so that his head is higher than the rest of his body (this will enable you to have eye contact with him and help encourage a smile) or hold the baby against your chest so that his head rests on your shoulder and is supported by one hand, with the other supporting his bottom.

When picking up a small baby, first slide one hand under his neck to support the head. Then slide the other hand under his back, and lift him gently into one of the carrying positions. Follow the diagram on page 8.

A sling is an excellent way of carrying a baby around. There are many styles on the market. Be sure the one you choose has adequate support for the baby's head, and you must ensure that he cannot slip out. A sling is generally best worn on the chest. That way, the baby can be seen most easily, and there is face-to-face contact again, but a backpack is also suitable for a slightly older infant. An older baby can be carried either on your hip or in front of you, with one hand around his waist and the other under him. Experiment with various carrying methods until you find one that is most comfortable and not too much of a strain.

Diaper dexterity

You will find there are so many types of diaper on the market that changing a baby is no longer the chore it used to be. Disposables are especially useful for traveling, and you will probably find them particularly handy to use when babysitting. All you need to remember is that it is pretty pointless changing a baby *before* a feeding, as he will probably be wet again very soon. Nor should you think that every time a baby cries he nees to be changed. He may just feel like a cuddle, he may be in discomfort or anxious for some other reason, or he may be hungry. The illustrations featured on

A new role

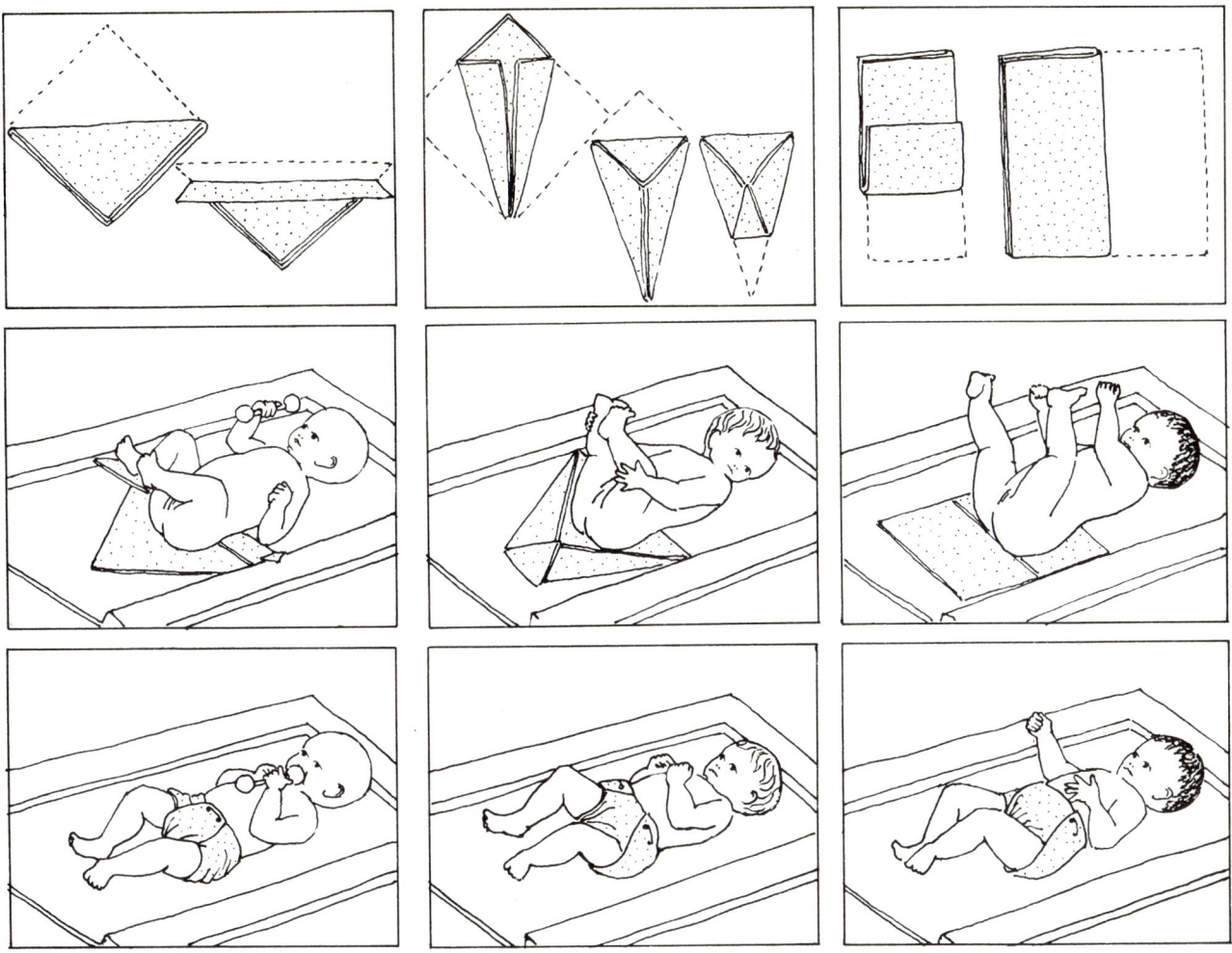

Unless you use pre-shaped diapers, you will need to become quite adept again at folding the fabric sort. But the knack is soon relearned. There are three principal methods, as shown in the illustrations here. The diaper can be folded into what is basically a triangular shape, for which you will need one pin, or a kite shape, or an oblong, for both of which two pins are needed. Remember when using the oblong method to put a baby girl on the thicker part of the folded diaper because this area will get wetter.

this page, show how to put on a diaper three different ways. Pre-shaped diapers, of course, make the task very much more simple.

There is no need to panic if you spot signs of diaper rash. Even the most coddled babies get sore from time to time, breastfed babies less frequently. The best solution is prevention, and a few simple steps will help greatly. Soft, well-rinsed diapers will help enormously as a precaution, as will the use of baby oil or lotion at the first sign of any soreness. Wash the baby's bottom gently but thoroughly before applying any ointments. You should also do everything possible to avoid letting the baby remain for long periods in a wet diaper. If possible, remove the diaper entirely; exposure to air will help the skin return to normal. The use of zinc and castor oil cream or petroleum jelly may also help not only to prevent but also to treat soreness by creating a barrier.

Feeding with a bottle

Make sure before you begin to feed that you are relaxed and comfortable, for the baby needs to be comfortable, too, if feeding is to be satisfactory. A chair of suitable height will also help because you will need to keep the baby's head raised during feeding. Hold him almost as if you were breastfeeding (no matter if you are a grandfather!) but just a little lower. Tilt the bottle so that the nipple is always full of milk. This will keep the baby from swallowing a lot of air. Never leave the baby alone to suck from a propped bottle; this can be very dangerous. Hygiene is also vitally important as far as bottle-feeding is concerned, and you will need to sterilize all equipment. Instructions for making up the feeding will be on the formula packaging and, no doubt, also left for you.

A new role

Bathing your new grandchild

Most parents like to bathe a baby every day, but this is not actually essential. 'Topping and tailing' – washing his head, face, and bottom only – may be adequate. A full bath can then be given every two or three days. Very small babies do not seem to like being bathed, and it is important to hold them securely in order to instill confidence. The bath should also be given fairly quickly so that he will not get cold. An infant's body temperature mechanism is not yet in full operation. The diagrams, shown below, illustrate how best to hold your small grandchild when bathing him. To ensure that bathtime goes smoothly, remember to:

- run the cold water first, and test the temperature with your elbow; it should be warm, not hot.
- prepare everything beforehand, so that there is no need to rush elsewhere midstream for equipment; and have all containers open, ready for you to use.
- make sure the room is warm.
- have a chair or stool to sit on.
- have ready on your lap a warm towel in which to wrap the baby as soon as he is undressed.
- clean his face with a special cloth. Do not poke anything into his ears. Dry his face.
- wash his hair gently while holding him over the bath and supporting him well.
- cover any hot taps with a cloth to prevent scalding.
- unwrap him from the towel and, holding him in your left hand, soap him. Lower him into the tub, and use your right hand to rinse him but take special care as his body will be slippery.
- lift him out of the water with both hands, and dry him well.
- never leave the baby alone in the bath.
- use a little baby oil or talcum powder, then dress him quickly so that he does not get cold.

Growth and development

Undoubtedly, one of the greatest pleasures of grandparenthood is watching your grandchild grow and develop. What delight you will find in his or her first smile, his first steps, and early baby talk! The most important thing to remember, however, is that not all children develop at the same rate. While your neighbor's grandchild may be sitting up at eight months, your own may not yet have reached that stage. This is not to say he is backward. He may in fact be advanced in other areas of development. Such small differences are unimportant. Some children are slow to walk and quick to talk, or vice versa. The average ages given for various developmental stages in medical textbooks are merely guidelines. The following is therefore intended only as a nonspecific timetable as to approximately when you might expect certain major milestones in your grandchild's development over the first three years to occur.

At birth watch for his early reflexes, particularly the walking reflex, soon lost, when he is held upright with feet on a flat surface. He can also grasp well in a reflex action and usually keeps his hands clenched.

At one month he may lift his head momentarily, sometimes stretch out his legs. He still spends most of his day sleeping.

At two months he can lift his head to a distinct angle and stretch himself out, his hands stay open for a longer time with fingers splayed, his eyes fix on an object that interests him, he may smile when picked up, and he grunts and coos.

At three months, now able to stretch himself out fully, he can also hold up his head for a longer period of time, and he squeals and gurgles. He will watch his hands as he plays with them.

A detailed revision course in how to bathe a small baby is provided in this chapter. Use small pieces of damp cotton swabs to clean your grandchild's face, wiping with a fresh piece for each eye from the nose to the outside of each eye. Support his head securely as you hold him over the bath and wash his hair. Make sure he is well supported, too, when in the bath. Dry him well and keep him warm. Use talcum powder only sparingly.

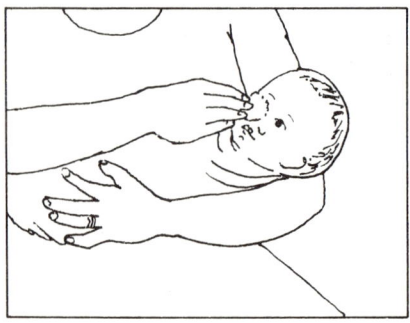
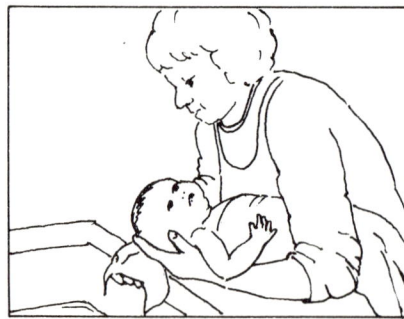
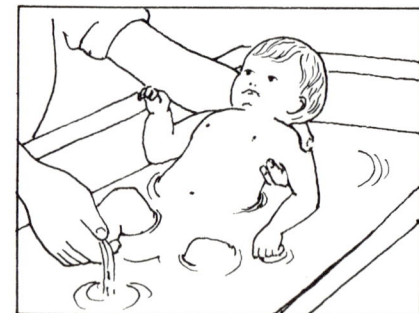

A new role

Make the most of the possibilities your grandparenting years offer. Time spent with the new generation can be enormous fun and also tremendously rewarding for grandparents and grandchildren alike. Remember, though, that toddlers can be exhausting company and that, if your grandchild comes to stay for a while, his visit will require some careful planning if you and he or she are to benefit to the full.

At four months, developing rapidly, he can roll onto his back, support himself on his forearms, and plays a lot with his hands. He can also now focus well at almost any distance, and will follow objects in any direction with his eyes.

At five months he is able to roll from his back onto his side, can grasp objects in both hands, and may try to put his feet in his mouth. Watch that he does not fall when he is rolling.

At six months he can roll freely and may sit up unsupported for a while, and for longer if propped up; he enjoys playing peek-a-boo and chatters with indistinguishable sounds. You may be able to hold him in a standing position.

At seven months his sitting ability is improving but still a little wobbly, he can hold objects securely, and is starting to make sounds like "ba", "da" and "ma".

At eight months he can sit up unsupported, and he uses his hands well. But keep a careful eye on him, because he may still topple at times.

At nine months he is begining to crawl, and can understand words like "no" and "bye-bye". Don't be too surprised if he tries to crawl backwards at first.

At ten months he tries to stand and walk, after crawling with straight arms and legs. Notice how he tries to pull himself up when he can.

At eleven months or more he is starting to walk with help, but crawling is still possibly his main method of moving. He may say one or two words you recognize, but is generally still babbling.

By 18 months word joining may begin (for example, "Mommy come"); he can probably stand and walk unaided, may be able to build a small tower of bricks, can use a spoon and turn over pages in a book, can recognize certain pictures and say the appropriate words, will fetch or show you something, if you ask him to do so, can say "bye-bye" and give you a kiss. He may also have made a lot of progress in getting his own way.

By 2 years he can open a door and perhaps unscrew a lid, can walk up and down stairs, one step at a time, may be able to put on certain garments himself, can scribble well, will correctly repeat words, can run and kick a ball, makes an attempt at washing his hands, is at the age of temper tantrums, enjoys 'helping' you, and is not happy to share toys. Gentle toilet training can start, but do not expect this to be successful too quickly.

By 3 years he can ride a tricycle, walks up and down stairs more proficiently, builds with bricks well, draws recognizable shapes, dresses himself well, constantly asks questions, can count to ten, perhaps knows nursery rhymes, perhaps joins a play group, and enjoys the stories you tell him enormously.

A new role

The adoptive grandparent

Not everyone becomes a grandparent because his or her children give birth. Some people suddenly find themselves grandparents because their children adopt children or undertake short-term fostering arrangements. Sometimes the transition can be pretty sudden. The shortest 'pregnancy' I know of lasted only half an hour. The adoption society called the prospective parents with the startling news that, following a lengthy waiting period, they at last had a baby for them. So suddenly, with only thirty minutes notice for everyone, there were two new parents and also four new grandparents.

The extent to which an adoptive grandparent may have to adapt should not be minimized. In addition to coming to terms with becoming a grandparent and getting to know the newborn infant, the adoptive grandparents may find it hard at first to accept the reality that there will be no 'natural' grandchild to continue an unbroken family line if infertility was the reason for adoption. The desire to have grandchildren is likely to be strong – so strong, sometimes, that adoptive grandparents, like parents, virtually have to mourn the loss of the baby that was never actually conceived.

Taking on the role of grandparent in these circumstances may require all the family spirit and goodwill that can be mustered, all the more so if the baby is of a different race or color. Such adaptation inevitably takes a little time and working at, but it will certainly pay dividends. It will also prove easier if you have discussed the prospective adoption and shared the experience of other adoptive grandparents. That is why intrauterine adoption (knowledge of the adoption prior to birth) has a great deal to commend it, even if there is an element of risk that the mother may change her mind and choose to keep the baby, which always remains her option for the first months.

Some mothers are even able to breastfeed an adopted baby, although they had not previously borne a child. Despite such intimacy, it may still take a while for everyone to accept the baby as one of the family circle, and to learn to love him. But most biological grandparents and parents will admit to having sometimes had ambivalent feelings about their own flesh and blood during the early days. Parenthood, and grandparenthood, do not always come naturally. Both are roles you need to work at because success is not guaranteed just because of family ties.

You may find it heartbreaking at first to think of the circumstances of your newly adopted grandchild's birth. Perhaps you can't help wondering whether he will one day want to find his biological parents – and grandparents – and prefer them to his own. Yet one fact is clear. It is the parent, and the grandparent, who loves and cares for a child who will always be most important to him. Love, experience repeatedly shows, is stronger than biology.

His adoptive parents will welcome all the encouragement you can give, and your support will be all the more essential if the adopted child is no longer a newborn baby, for feelings of security may well be lacking if there has been an institutional background or a tragic family history of some kind.

Your adopted grandchild may bear no physical resemblance to the family, but a blood relation might not either. By the same token, there is no evidence at all that tendencies to alcoholism or delinquency, for instance, are hereditary. Ignore such doubts and settle down to enjoying your new role. Be proud of the tremendous social responsibility your children have taken on in adopting a family. It should be a rewarding decision for you all, if approached in a positive way. Your new grandchild's parents will be advised by the adoption society and counselors as to the best way to explain to the child himself about the adoption. Meanwhile, you may be able to help teach your grandchild something about the birthright of his own ethnic culture if he is of a different race; that is widely considered a particular responsibility of the adoptive family. Encourage the family to ask for advice from a counselor or from an adoption worker if any problems occur. This will not be taken as an indication of failure but as a mark of confidence and the will to succeed.

You may also become a grandparent overnight if one of your children marries someone with a ready-made family. As a step-grandparent, your role will be valuable, and you should find that you are warmly accepted, as long as the basic family situation is a healthy one. It is to be hoped that you will warmly accept him.

The tender trap

If you have, say, three children of your own and each has a family, the chances are you will have at least three grandchildren, maybe many more. Just as your own children probably differed in personality and appearance, to a greater or lesser extent, so your grandchildren will differ from each other. You may overhear them vigorously claiming that you love one better than another, just as you remember your own children did. Your immediate reaction should be to deny it and to reassure them that all are loved equally. If one child is made to feel better or superior at another's expense, particularly within one family unit, there could be

A new role

behavior hazards and emotional upsets in store. Try to distribute treats and presents with equal fairness, and to give praise to all at times. As for your own inner feelings, remember that no two loves are truly equal. A child, however, is unable to understand that it is possible to love in different ways, for different reasons, sometimes 'because of' and sometimes 'in spite of'. Each grandchild is bound to arouse a different emotional response in you, making you in many ways a different sort of grandparent to each of them. Each grandchild should be someone special in his or her own right.

If, by chance, you get off to a bad start with a grandchild (perhaps you had really hoped for a grandchild of another sex, perhaps he or she seemed rather ugly at first, or perhaps you are simply not at ease with small babies), it will require something of an effort on your part to make up for lost time. But you *can* do so, and the baby with whom you were once so uncomfortable may turn out to be a delightful child who thrives on your affection and whose company you soon come to adore.

Caring or spoiling?

That children thrive on attention and affection cannot be denied. But parents are often at pains to prevent grandparents from taking this to extremes, frequently accusing them of spoiling a child to his or her detriment.

The greatest danger, perhaps, lies in the relationship between grandparents and a youngest grandchild, often seen as the baby of the whole family. Yet, the truly spoilt child is rare, at least as far as grandparents are concerned, and parents often grossly misjudge the situation, commonly mistaking a more relaxed attitude for indulgent behavior.

The archetypal grandmother of Italian or Eastern European origin was often at fault, however, in seeming to equate food with love, forcing her grandchildren to eat large quantities of high-calorie food. But today, with so much emphasis placed on health education and preventive medicine, even older – and thus possibly very traditional grandparents – are unlikely to confuse the dietary and emotional aspects of a child's development.

As for demonstrative affection, you can do no better than to take your cues from your grandchild, remembering that the child who loved to sit on your knee at three may be embarrassed even to hold your hand in public by the age of seven. He needs to let go in the grandparent – grandchild relationship, just as he does in that with his parents. This is not to say that there are exacting rules about when to stop cuddling a child; there is no definite age. But the timing and

Playing together should help create a very valuable bond between you both.

nature of any changes should be tailored to his needs. As your grandchild grows, you will have to show your love in other ways.

Family relationships

The birth of your grandchild will herald a period rich with new experiences. You may find, for instance, that a daughter, once very anxious to appear independent and scornful of your opinions, suddenly approaches you for guidance and positively welcomes your participation in caring for the new baby. But if you are to maintain this newly improved and valued relationship, you will need to be careful right from the beginning not to overdo things on the advice front. In this respect, remember the advice that headed many school examination papers: *Answer only the questions asked.* Your advice should be to the point. Phraseology is also important and can prevent many a resentful rebuff. It is better to explain that you used to find this, that, or the other thing helpful than to give firm, authoritarian instructions, however well-intentioned these are.

Most of us need to remember as the grandchildren develop that many of the things our children do as parents reflect the way they themselves were brought up. Occasionally, however, because people dislike the way they were treated as a child, they may intentionally introduce very different methods of child rearing. On the whole, however, we are remarkably accurate in the way we repeat behavior patterns. To cite one example, I recall a mother coming to

A new role

see me about her child's diet. She mentioned that he repeatedly refused peas that she hid in the mashed potatoes. Only as she spoke did she recall that *her* mother, too, had for some mysterious reason insisted that she, as a child, should eat all her peas.

Children, on the whole, thoroughly enjoy the company of their grandparents. They love hearing about the past, and you have an important role in the passing on of family traditions. A grandfather often finds he has far more free time to spend with his grandchildren than he had many years ago for his own children; work may be less high-pressure or he may be retired. Interfamily rivalries are to be avoided at all costs. There is no need to be jealous that the 'other side' sees the grandchildren more often. If such a situation does arise, make the most of the occasions when you have the grandchildren, mention that you would like to see more of them, and await response. It may just be a matter of geographical location or other practical considerations.

Even if you live some distance from the grandchildren, it is still possible to maintain regular contact by letter or by telephone and thus fulfil your role as grandparent. Children love receiving mail and, after the age of three or four, are usually quite competent on the telephone. The grandparent residing several thousand miles away can instil a feeling of security in a child by keeping in regular contact. For neither rearing nor being a child is easy or straightforward, and your supportive role will be appreciated by parents and youngsters alike. Those of us fortunate enough to remember our own grandparents usually do so with great affection. Looking ahead, it seems that pure economics could perhaps dictate a return to the extended family, with all the very positive benefits this can bring.

Taking an active interest

Even if you are not able to see your grandchild all that often, you will still want to inquire regularly about his progress and thus maintain an active interest. These early months are precious, and it would be a pity not to share in the joy they can bring. But not everything goes smoothly all the time, and there are bound to be difficulties occasionally – family conflicts or developmental or emotional problems, perhaps. (We take a look at some quite common examples on pages 76 – 81.) No one is alone in such experiences. But it is very often a grandparent who, being one step removed, can maintain a sense of perspective and help keep the family on a fairly even keel. A gentle, kindly word –not smothering advice – can sometimes work absolute wonders.

Your active interest may also be welcomed, on a very practical level. If your daughter or daughter-in-law is taking the baby to the clinic for a checkup, for instance, you could assist by driving or by simply accompanying her there. Your presence may be reassuring; but, of course, do ask first! You may like to offer to play host for a birthday party or to arrange a special treat or outing. You may want to attend an openhouse or sports event at your grandchild's school. In this respect, the best offering you have to give is *time*. Find time to cradle your grandchildren and later to talk to them, to walk with them and read to them, to answer their questions, however incessant and seemingly absurd they are at times. Find time to ask about their hobbies and progress at school, to lend an ear and wipe away a tear, to take an interest in *their* interests, and to tell them about their own parents as children. Your reward will be to see them positively blossom.

To everyone's benefit

Any boy or girl fortunate enough to have regular contact with his or her grandparents will certainly enjoy a greatly enriched childhood. The grandparent–grandchild relationship is, on the whole, a very valuable one, adding greatly to a youngster's feeling of security and providing many happy, satisfying hours for the grandparent, too.

You are bound to have a lot of fun together, but your presence may be important on another level as well, instilling in the child a sense of respect for the elderly. For a while you may still be young chronologically, you are "old" in his eyes, and contact with you will naturally provide his first experience of the ageing process and thus a first appreciation of the very nature of life.

At the same time, as the role of grandparent gradually becomes more familiar to you, you will be wise to ensure that in no way does the family take advantage of your enthusiasm. That can easily happen. As in all relationships, there has to be give and take. Sometimes it may simply not be convenient for you to babysit; you must say so. The chances are that the family will be able to make perfectly suitable alternative arrangements, and the next time you help out, you will be appreciated all the more. And if, at times, you simply find the grandchildren too much of a handful (perhaps you are not that fit, and they are rather boisterous), then it really is important that you say so, for the children's well-being, as well as your own.

Make the most of your grandparenting years. The potential is enormous. With the blessings of good fortune and good health, many of us may enjoy great-grandparenthood, too.

Hugh Jolly

What are grandparents for?

This question was put to a group of children aged between seven and thirteen, from seven different countries. Here are some of their answers.

- A grandmother is a lady who has no children of her own and therefore she loves other people's little boys and girls.

- Grandmothers don't do anything, they just need to be there. They never say, 'Come quickly' or 'Hurry up, for heaven's sake.'

- They are fat, but not too fat to do up our shoelaces. They wear glasses and sometimes they are able to pull out your tooth.

- They know the answers to questions like 'Why do dogs hate cats' and 'Why isn't God married?'

- When they read us a story, they never skip any pages and they don't mind if it is always the same story.

- Everybody should have a grandmother, especially if you don't have television.

- Grandmothers are the only grown-ups who always have time for you.

- Grandma always thinks of us and telephones us. She always plays games with us. Grandmothers have their limits, they send us to bed and don't give us any sweets before supper.

- Grandfathers have no limits, they just want us to have a good time.

- They see to it that our mothers behave themselves.

From **Listen to the Children**
compiled by Annejet Campbell

Guess who's coming to stay!

While a child is very small, he is happiest in his usual home environment; so if you have to look after him while his parents are away, it may be best if *you* can visit. Since this will not always be possible, however, you may find yourself playing host to your young grandchild, either overnight or for several days.

It will be a very special time for you when your grandchild first comes to stay, particularly if he comes without his parents. It could also be the first time he has ever been away from home, so you may have to be especially understanding if he or she seems a little homesick at first. This is only natural.

Your grandchild's parents should definitely explain to him, if he is old enough to understand, precisely why and for how long he will be staying with you, in order to reassure him that they have not gone off, never to reappear. They should also go out of their way to maintain contact by telephone, if the child seems particularly upset.

A certain amount of advance planning on your part is required if the visit is to go smoothly, especially if it has been a long time since you last had a toddler about the house. But first you will need to reassure your grandchild's parents that you are capable of looking after a young child. If you are at all infirm, you ought to think twice about having a boisterous youngster to stay because looking after a child can be exhausting if you are not used to it, even at the best of times.

In other sections of this book, you will find many helpful ideas for outings and treats, as well as for things to make and games to play. Safety aspects and first aid hints are featured, and several pages of recipes offer suggestions for making interesting meals for your grandchildren.

Cooking for your grandchild

If you plan to cook special meals for your grandchild, you will probably want to see them enjoyed. It will be wise, therefore, to check up on any food likes and dislikes, as well as any allergies. Faced with a finicky eater, however, you may have to resort to a few meal-time tricks. If your

There are certain safety aspects you will need to check up on, now that you are likely to have young visitors from time to time. Never leave a toddler alone in the kitchen. He will be keen to explore, so remember not to leave anything around which you would prefer him not to touch. At bedtime, too, have safety in mind. A small baby should not be given a pillow, remember, while a toddler may find a favorite toy a source of comfort when away from home.

Guess who's coming to stay!

grandchild likes only hamburgers or fish sticks, you could perhaps serve these for one or two meals, but the visit may provide him or her with a wonderful opportunity to experiment with new dishes. The chances are that this will be all the more successful if you can make the menu not only well-balanced nutritionally but also visually exciting. An ordinary portion of peas can look very dull, but if you arrange them on some mashed potatoes to form a face, you may find they will be better received.

Don't give too many filling snacks between meals so that, when it comes to lunch or dinner, your grandchild still has a healthy appetite. Home-made snacks are usually preferable to commercial, oversweet products, so that it will be a good idea to bake a few cookies in advance of your grandchild's arrival. Fruit makes an excellent snack, too. It is unwise, however, to give peanuts. They can be dangerous if not swallowed properly.

Think twice before serving anything very highly spiced, unless you know for certain that the young palate is accustomed to such flavoring.

It is definitely a good idea, particularly with a fussy eater, to keep portions small and then to offer more. Loss of appetite may be due to illness or emotional disturbance for some reason, or simply to the fact that your grandchild is not hungry. Don't get too tense about meals, and problems will probably disappear. Children generally eat when they need to, and constant food refusal is very rare. Your grandchild will eat when hunger demands it, never fear.

You will probably want your toddler grandchild to wear a bib when eating. The most practical ones are made of plastic, and have a lip to catch whatever is dropped. Have some napkins and paper towels handy, too, at mealtimes. Use a plastic cup rather than a glass one that might break if he bites it. Cover a good, wooden table with a plastic cloth or serve on a surface that can be wiped easily. If you get more than a little frustrated at times with spoon-feeding, you may like to offer finger foods so that your grandchild can try feeding himself with small slices of bread or pieces of ripe banana, for instance. A carrot stick will provide excellent chewing exercise for the developing teeth and jaw.

If your grandchild is very young, you will have to bottle-feed him. His mother may have left a bottle of her own breast milk at first: thereafter, use a formula, not ordinary milk, which is unsuitable for new babies. Make up the formula exactly according to the instructions, using *boiled* water, and mix thoroughly. Don't increase the strength of the feeding: this can be dangerous. The bottle doesn't have to be warm, but it should not be too cold. You can heat a feeding by standing the bottle in a pitcher of hot water or by running hot water over the bottle. Then test the temperature by shaking a few drops onto your wrist. Sterilization of the equipment you use is very important.

When bottle-feeding, make sure you are sitting comfortably, and hold your grandchild in a half-upright position, turned towards you. Change from one arm to the other for comfort. If you have to give your grandchild any supplements or medicines that have been prescribed, make a note each time they are taken so that you do not give them twice.

Guess who's coming to stay!

Bathtime tips

Giving a lively baby or toddler a bath doesn't have to be too strenuous if you take things calmly and prepare well in advance. Turn to page 14 for a revision course in bathtime basics. Here are some further useful tips, too. First of all, try to make bathtime fun for your grandchild by introducing toys into the water. Have everything you need nearby so that there will be no need to leave your young grandchild alone in the bathroom. Don't use a lot of water, even in a small baby bath, and lift your grandchild into the tub with a straight back and bent knees, to avoid undue strain on yourself. Certain important points of hygiene need emphasizing. Cleanse his or her eyes with cotton swabs, using a different piece for each eye, and take care not to put anything into his or her ears. When cleaning the diaper area, wipe a baby girl from the front towards the anus and don't pull back an uncircumcised baby boy's foreskin for cleaning until it has separated. Remember to keep your grandchild warm, too, and to dry him or her carefully and quickly, using baby powder very sparingly.

Disposable diapers will be most convenient for you to use, but if you prefer the cloth kind, use a diaper liner so that any heavy soiling can be easily removed. Whether you wash cloth diapers yourself or send them to a diaper service, soak them first in sterilizing solution so that the risk of diaper rash is minimized. It's best to change a baby's diaper *after* a feeding rather than before, remember.

Bedtime procedures

Children need regular sleeping patterns, so try to follow your grandchild's usual bedtime routine. Since he will be sleeping in a strange bed, have him bring along a favorite toy or blanket. Warm the bed with a hot water bottle for a while, removing it before he gets in, and make sure that the room itself is sufficiently warm but not stuffy.

Try not to let your grandchild get too excited before he goes to bed because that may make it difficult for him to get off to sleep. Children love bedtime rituals; so a bath, a story, and perhaps a lullaby will almost certainly be appreciated. If a child is really not tired enough to sleep, you can get him ready for bed and let him come downstairs. That way, you won't have to undress him when he does get sleepy.

A newborn baby actually sleeps on the average more than twenty hours out of every twenty-four, but in intermittent periods. By the time he is two, a child generally needs about twelve hours sleep at night, and an hour or two during the day, but sleep needs vary and some children seem to need considerably less rest than most. However, an older overtired child often finds it difficult to get to sleep, so he may still need that afternoon nap.

A warm bath, a soothing drink, a lullaby, rocking, a bedtime story, and a goodnight kiss will all help get a small baby or toddler off to sleep. Put an infant grandchild down on his right or left side, or on his front, and never give a pillow. Particularly if this is the first time your young grandchild has come to stay, in fact whatever his age, never lock the door to the room in which he is sleeping. Leave it ajar and show him where *your* room is just in case he is frightened or needs something in the night.

If your grandchild tries delaying tactics because he does not want to go to sleep – perhaps by asking repeatedly for a glass of water or calling for company, complaining he is too hot or wanting to go to the bathroom yet again – it often works wonders if you promise to come back again in a few minutes. You must, of course, actually do so. When you do, you will probably find he has already dozed off, relaxed and comforted by your promise.

All children have bad dreams at times. Because the occasional nightmare is perfectly normal, there should be no need to worry unduly if your grandchild has this experience while staying with you. If he does have a bad dream don't criticize him for disturbing you or for making a fuss. Instead, stay with him and offer all the comfort you can, explaining that everything is the same as it was when he went to bed and that it was merely a silly dream. If he is prone to wandering at night, you may need to consider a gate at the top of the stairs, just as his parents will probably have done. A night light can be helpful for the particularly nervous child. Repeated waking during the night may be due to any one of a number of factors: a frightening book or television program, disturbance to daily routine, worry about school, or even wetting the bed.

If bedwetting is sometimes a problem, leave a toddler in a diaper and plastic pants for the night. See that he visits the bathroom before going to bed, and perhaps again when you retire for the night. You cannot be completely sure that a child will be dry at night before the age of four, so do not expect too much from your grandchild. Once he is dry, however, any sudden lapse can usually be traced to an emotional cause, such as moving to a new house or a new sibling in the family. Keep a change of sheets and nightclothes handy if you know from experience that he may wet the bed. Above all, do everything you can not to let him feel too upset or embarrassed about it.

If your grandchild tends to wake early and you don't want to be disturbed, leave him a few toys and books with which he can play until you get up. Never give him a sedative for this reason, nor at any time without a doctor's prescription, for that matter. You might also leave a breakfast snack for him either in the bedroom or in the kitchen, if he is old enough to be trusted there on his own: but it would be wise not to let him use the stove without supervision.

Coping for themselves

Although most three-year-olds can dress and undress themselves, if a bit clumsily, they may still need help. However, let your grandchild get as far as he can on his own. Don't hurry him or her unless you really have to do so. You can then add the finishing touches. The prospect of dressing a small baby often seems daunting and you may feel awkward at first, but you will soon get used to it again. Use a flat surface – a bed or a special changing mat are ideal. Small babies should be dressed quite quickly so that they do not get too cold.

Why is he crying?

Hearing your infant grandchild cry and not fully understanding why can be very disturbing. A mother soon learns to distinguish her baby's different cries. But as a grandparent, you will be less familiar with them unless you are around for most of the time. A baby's crying is his only means of communication. It can indicate, among other things, discomfort, thirst, that he is too hot, hungry, or simply that he needs a cuddle. Don't get agitated either, for a unhappy state of mind on your part could easily disturb him all the more. Babies are exceptionally good indicators on the whole of the state of mind of their mothers or whoever is looking after them.

Baby talk

It takes time for toddlers to master the art of communication by speech, and it is perfectly normal for them to have a language of their own for quite some while. The mother who is constantly with her child naturally comes to understand the meaning of most of those cooings and gurglings: but relatives and friends, because they are not so often with the child, usually find it a little more difficult. By the age of eighteen months, most children can say at least six words, and by three will try using sentences. Some children are rather more slow to speak, however. Before your small grandchild comes to stay, ask his parents whether he has any special vocabulary of his own. You may find, for instance, that for some mysterious reason a sound like 'goo' or 'ma' means milk. Talk to your infant grandchild, even though he will respond only with coos. Your attempts at conversation will help his early speech enormously. Try, too, not to use 'baby talk' when speaking with him. There really is no need to call a dog a 'bow-wow' or to use other substitute words in this way.

A matter of routine

Small children, just like many adults, come to rely on routine to a very great extent for a sense of safety. Knowing what to expect gives them confidence. Before your grandchild comes to stay, therefore, try to find out what the pattern of his day is normally like when he or she is at home, so that changes can be kept to a minimum. This is not to say that you must adapt your own daily timetable to his or her routine entirely. Older children will benefit from experiencing a new environment, and will probably find it enjoyable to be doing things slightly differently, if your daily way of life is not quite the same as that of their parents. But do try not to let any element of change be so great that a child feels uncomfortable.

Getting organized

If a visit is to be successful, it has to be planned to some extent. But whatever outings you may have in mind, do be sure to have some alternative plans, just in case the weather lets you down. There is nothing worse than having a bored child about the house, nagging for something to do. But the visit should not be one long treat. Away from home, your grandchild may actually enjoy helping with setting the table and straightening up, although washing dishes may not be such a good idea because of the risk of breakages. Assisting with simple cooking can also be an enjoyable activity for four and five-year-olds, girls *and* boys.

If your grandchild is used to helping about the house, let him help you, too, during his stay. You may even find that the child who is unwilling to help at home actually volunteers to do so when away. If he tries to make a good impression in this way, don't refuse his offers of assistance by insisting that you can cope: that would be tantamount to a rejection. Take advantage of his help! Not all children are always so cooperative.

Gentle encouragement for the child who does not offer help of his own accord would also not go amiss. Let him help you sweep up or clean the car. Even if it does not amount to very practical assistance at first, you will be laying good foundations for the future.

Organization is the keyword when it comes to having grandchildren to stay with you, whether simply for a weekend or for longer. Plan the visit carefully, and you and this very special houseguest should both have a wonderful time.

Guess who's coming to stay!

Coping with twins

If you are fortunate enough to have twin grandchildren, you are no doubt particularly proud of them. Whether identical or not, twins are always delightful. But on a practical level, if you are ever asked to look after them for a while, you really ought to consider very carefully whether you could cope. Two grandparents might be able to manage: otherwise you will probably need some additional help, if only because it will be very difficult indeed for anyone not used to caring for two small babies to handle both at once. Having twin grandchildren may be a double blessing, but it may also mean double the trouble when they come to stay.

Too much television?

During your grandchild's visit, you may find yourself wondering whether he or she should be watching quite so much television. If this is the case, you will obviously need to consider very carefully whether you are providing enough by way of stimulating activity. Children get bored very quickly indeed, so you will need to think up quite a number of ideas and projects to keep him or her fully occupied. However, current medical opinion seems to be that, contrary to what was once thought, television is unlikely to harm the eyes. (Your may remember that many years ago, reading was thought to be harmful in this way, too). Many television programs especially for children are quite likely to be entertaining and also have a high educational content. You will probably enjoy watching these shows with your grandchild. Make the most of them by discussing them together afterwards, too. But, of course, you may need to censor those programs obviously only suitable for adult viewers by virtue of their subject matter. It will be wise, too, to see that your grandchild does not watch any very frightening productions before he goes to bed if he is of a nervous disposition.

Making new friends

It will be an excellent idea if you can introduce your grandchild to some of your neighbors' children of a similar age group while he is staying with you. The company of other children will be welcome, and a few hours relaxation while he goes to their house or apartment will be of benefit to you, too. Many friendships between children can start in this way. They might begin to exchange letters, as well as birthday and Christmas cards, and your grandchild will probably look forward to his next visit to you even more if there is the added attraction of a friend to play with, too.

Temper tantrums

Most children have a temper tantrum at one time or another: but when it happens, it still usually comes as something of a disturbing experience – to both adult and child alike. You may remember your own children behaving in this way; and more recently will no doubt have seen examples when out and about, if not in your own grandchild. One of the most common places for this to occur is in the supermarket, possibly because the child is upset by the crowds, tired and utterly bored. But a tantrum can, of course, also occur in a domestic situation. The young child, his needs totally frustrated, cannot express himself and seems to burst with fury. If this ever happens when your grandchild comes to stay, there are two alternative approaches you can use which parents sometimes say they find effective with different children. One is not to lose control yourself and react by being angry, but to get down to the child's level and to comfort him, because the chances are he is finding his own behavior quite upsetting. The other approach, where you feel that the tantrum is being put on as something of a test of your breaking point, is to ignore the behavior. You may be wise to ask your grandchild's parents if he is likely to behave in this way at all and, if so, which sort of approach they have used successfully.

Guess who's coming to stay!

Of course, you may be able to cope admirably when your grandchildren come to stay. But if it is a while since you last looked after an infant, be wary of taking on too much. Twins, for instance, may prove a handful. You will also be wise not to leave too many ornaments on display. Accidents do happen when lively toddlers are around. Remember, too, that your grandchild may need help with getting dressed.

If you are unwell

Should you ever be looking after an infant grandchild on your own, it will be very sensible to ask a neighbour or relative to telephone you or call by at least once during the day, just in case of a mishap. The older we are, the more prone we are to falls or illnesses: and a baby might, in such circumstances, be in great distress. You should also see that an older grandchild knows how to telephone for an ambulance and what information he should give. This is a very wise precaution to take in advance of the visit. It will always be a good idea, too, to keep a list of emergency numbers by your telephone.

As an additional safety precaution, you should take every step to ensure that there are no drugs or medicines lying about within reach of your grandchild. So many of these look like candies, and a toddler may be tempted to try them. In particular, do not leave any pills on the floor by the side of your bed as many people do. They may easily be picked up by your grandchild if he is crawling, and his curiosity may get the better of him. Be sure, too, not to lift your grandchild if you are suffering from a bad back or some other condition that requires you to be careful. When reaching down to him or her, bend your knees rather than stooping, as you should do whenever you have to get to anything at floor level.

Is it allowed?

Very commonly when they are away from home, children will try to get their own way by saying that their parents would agree. If your grandchildren comes to stay, you may well find this happening with requests for candy or chocolate, for instance, or with demands to stay up late. Before the visit, it will therefore be wise to check with his parents on any codes of behavior they have set down and on any family 'rules'. In practice, you will probably find that you have to be quite firm in stating that you know that his parents do not permit this if your grandchild starts nagging for something, since it will cearly be very wrong to go against their wishes and thus to create a conflict.

Keeping a record

On pages 92-95, you will find a facility for keeping notes about each grandchild's special likes and dislikes, any allergies to foods, hobbies and interests, and emergency telephone numbers. Complete this useful memorandum so that you have readily to hand a record of all such important information for when your young visitors come to stay. If you have more than four grandchildren, simply insert an additional loose-leaf page for each.

Safety Steps

As your grandchild develops, and particularly once he is crawling and up on his own two feet, his curiosity increases. When he comes to visit for an afternoon, or perhaps for a longer stay, you will need to be very careful about the risk of accidents because, now that he is so active, he is bound to find exploring your home something of an adventure. For many years, your house or apartment has probably been perfectly safe for adults. But you will have to be several steps ahead of your grandchild, and constantly aware of where he is and what he might reach, if you are to keep him out of harm's way. When you are out with your young charge, too, you will need to be constantly safety conscious. A toddler, particularly, may wander off, if you do not keep watch on him.

Out and about

The annual statistics for children involved in road accidents are absolutely terrifying. What is more, a large proportion of injured children are under five years of age; so it is never too early to instill traffic sense. As a general guideline, children under five years of age should not be allowed to cross any street on their own. They are far too easily distracted and cannot yet judge speed or anticipate a driver's reaction. Teach your grandchild by example. Whenever you are out together, use pedestrian crossings and traffic lights. Show him or her how to look around and to listen for traffic. Teach him, too, never to dart out from behind a parked car because of the risk of an accident caused by oncoming traffic. While he is very small, if he is not in a stroller, you might want to consider using a harness or leash.

If you have bought him a tricycle, be sure that either you or his parents set down some rules. A tricycle is never meant to be ridden in the street. Your grandchild could be in extreme danger if he does so, since he will be far too low to be spotted easily by a driver. He should ride it either in the yard or in a park, but if you allow him on the sidewalk, be sure he rides steadily and keeps away from the curb. Once he has a bicycle, and that could be as early as five years old, you will need to be additionally careful. The model chosen should have passed all the necessary safety tests, if new; if second-hand, it should be carefully looked at for faults. Never allow a young child in the street with a bicycle. He may want to show off; but unless you live in a town with special cycle lanes, he could be in great danger. He may be allowed to ride it in the park, but will have to push it there and back, walking on the sidewalk. He should not ride at all when it is dark, but see that his lights are working, just in case. The wearing of a reflective band and other luminous clothing is an additional safety precaution.

In the living-room

Make sure there are no electric cords to trip anyone up, and install a fireguard if necessary. Use safety plugs when electrical sockets are not in use. For your own sake, keep any valuable fragile ornaments out of the way. Don't leave cigarettes lying around (either in a package or smoked ones in an ashtray). If a small child swallows one, it could be dangerous. Alcohol can be lethal for a baby, too, so keep it out of reach – best of all, locked away so that a child cannot get at it.

Kitchen safety

Your grandchild is probably most vulnerable to accidents in the kitchen, so special care is required here. Lock up all cleaning aids, and never be tempted to pour household poisons into other containers. Bleach in an old lemonade bottle, for instance, could prove highly dangerous if mistaken for a drink. Keep chairs and stools away from the stove, and turn all pot and pan handles towards the back. Remember to keep an infant out of the way when you are using hot water or serving meals, and never pass hot food or drinks over him. A child can be easily scalded in this way. Spills can also cause slipping. All plastic bags, matches, and lighters should be put away. Everything sharp should be well out of reach of a toddler, and children should not be playing at your feet when you are busy in the kitchen, either ironing or cooking.

Safely tucked up

All nightwear should be flame resistant. Never use a pillow in a small baby's crib or buggy, for fear of suffocation, and remove his bib before you lay him down. Don't leave a pacifier tied around his neck on a long ribbon. If you're making a hot water bottle for a child, be sure the water is not so hot that it will scald him if it leaks; use it only to warm the bed. A crib with rails that cannot possibly permit a baby's head to pass through them is a necessity; nontoxic paint should be used on the crib, and there should be no large gap between the mattress and the crib sides. A toy-strewn floor in a nursery may be dangerous, too, and could trip *you* up. Remember not to keep your own drugs and medicines in or on a cabinet by your bedside, where they will be within easy reach of your grandchild. They could be lethal to a toddler.

In the bathroom

All medicines should be safely locked away. Cleaning fluids should also be out of reach, don't leave razor blades lying about, and see that a bath mat is not left on a slippery floor. Never use a portable electric appliance in the bathroom, and see that any heater you have is high up on the wall. When preparing a bath for your grandchild, run the cold water first, before adding the hot, to prevent scalds. Never leave a small child alone in the bath, and use a safety mat. A large, firm sponge is far better than small, soft one that a baby may be tempted to put in his mouth and on which he may choke. Use talcum powder rather sparingly; it can be inhaled and may block air passages. Make sure, too, that the lock on the door is quite high up and not used by a child, or that it can be opened with a coin from the outside. Once he or she is so independent that complete privacy is required in the bathroom, simply assure your grandchild that you will not disturb him or her, and that there is no real need to lock the door in case it gets stuck.

Windows, stairs and doors

If your small grandchild is likely to be upstairs at all, it will be wise to fix and use safety catches on all accessible windows. Bars or gates on particularly approachable windows might be an additional sensible precaution. Whenever you have to be in another part of the house, use of a safety gate at the top and bottom, of the stairs is another good precaution, but do encourage your grandchild to learn how to cope with stairs. He may need a helping hand at first, even if he is quite used to them in his own home, because they may be rather steeper or incline at a different angle. It's not a good idea, either from a child's standpoint or from yours, to have a loose rug or mat at the bottom of the stairs which may easily cause someone to trip. If you have highly polished floors, it is dangerous for a child to run around in socks, as this may turn the floor into a veritable skating rink. Sliding down the banisters, you may have to explain, simply is not done because of the tremendous risks involved. Check that your stairs are well lit for reasons of safety, too.

Outdoors

Make sure you have no old equipment lying around, which might provide a dangerous hiding place. There should be no ready access to the street and any gates, front and back, should be kept closed and preferably locked. Garden ponds, attractive as they are, can be quite dangerous when children are around. Cover them with a good strong mesh netting. If you have a swimming pool or provide a paddling area in the summer, be sure that an adult is on hand, to supervise play. It only takes a couple of inches of water to drown a small child.

Keep the garage and tool shed locked, and see that dangerous tools and poisons such as paraffin, weed-killer, and insect sprays are stored so that access by a child is impossible. Don't leave gardening equipment, such as a lawn mower, lying around either. Any baby left outdoors should also have his buggy protected with a net to keep out insects as far as possible as well as curious cats. Warn your grandchild about the dangers of eating berries, mushrooms, and plants in the yard.

The accident-prone child

Accidents can occur for a wide variety of reasons, as we have seen: and every possible care should be taken when small children are around. Some children, however, seem to have more then their fair share of accidents, continually falling over or breaking things. Indeed, the emergency rooms of hospitals are very much aware that certain children come back time and time again for treatment following mishaps. Many psychologists have pointed out that these accident-prone children are sometimes suffering from acute anxiety. So if you feel that this seems to be the case within your family circle, you might do well to consider whether there is an emotional problem of some kind. It may be, for instance, that your grandchild has been troubled by the birth of a new sister or brother.

As safe as houses

On the two pages that follow, you will find illustrated the principal safety measures to bear in mind in a domestic situation when toddlers are around. The old saying "as safe as houses" isn't valid where children are concerned unless you keep a eye open for hazards. But looking after a child doesn't have to be a nerve-racking experience, if you do your best to instill confidence in him. Spend time teaching him what to look out for and how to manage his environment safely. In this way, both his trust in you and his self-reliance will develop and flourish.

Safety at home

Safety at home

When your grandchild visits, you will need to be particularly careful about potential dangers. Although your home may be quite safe for adults, it could be hazardous to an infant or toddler. Check the safety points given below, and remind your grandchild's parents about them, too. Is your house or apartment as childproof as it should be?

In the kitchen and utility areas
1. Store your ironing board neatly. Don't iron with a toddler around.
2. Keep the washing machine closed.
3. Watch for dangerous spills and see that the floor and throw rugs are nonslip.
4. Consider fixing a safety guard to your stove.
5. Avoid clutter.
6. Turn all handles of pots and pans towards the back of the stove.
7. Consider fitting windows and doors with safety glass.
8. Keep matches, knives, and other such dangerous implements out of reach.
9. Be sure that all disinfectants and household poisons are stored out of reach or in a locked cupboard.
10. Don't let cords trail dangerously.
11. If you eat in the kitchen, keep your dining table well away from the cooking area.
12. Try to ensure that a window blind pulley is easy to get at, without reaching over a hot stove.
13. Keep all your electric equipment out of reach.
14. Perhaps have the telephone fixed to the wall.

In the bathroom
1. Use a safety mat in the bathtub.
2. Choose nonslip flooring.
3. Keep the medicine cabinet locked or medicines well out of reach.
4. Don't leave razor blades around.
5. Keep all cleaning materials out of reach.
6. Warn your grandchild about a hot towel rail.
7. Any additional heating should be ceiling mounted or high up on a wall. Monitor the use of electrical appliances (toothbrushes, blow dryers, radios, etc.)
8. Always run the cold tap before the hot tap.
9. Don't allow your grandchild to lock the door, in case of emergency. Tell him or her that you respect a closed door as much as a locked one.

28

Safety at home

10 A bolt is usually preferable to a key.
11 Use of a shower curtain should prevent a wet floor.
12 A pulley light will be safer than a switch in a bathroom.

The stairs
1 Check that there are no worn or ragged carpet edges.
2 All stairs should be well lit.
3 A safety gate at top and bottom may be a wise precaution if your small grandchild has the run of your house.
4 Avoid placing a mat at the bottom of the stairs.

The living-room
1 All open, gas, or electric fires should be protected by a guard.
2 It is wise to use safety plugs in the electrical outlets.
3 Trailing cords can cause falls.
4 Avoid displaying valuable ornaments, if your grandchild touches everything.
5 It will be wise to fix safety glass to internal doors or large patio windows.
6 Keep all alcohol locked away.
7 Do not leave cigarettes around.
8 Table mats will be preferable to a low hanging cloth which a crawling child might pull.
9 Beware of loose rugs.

In the bedroom
1 Do not give a small baby a pillow. Make sure, too, that the child cannot crawl out of his crib and that crib bars are spaced properly so his head cannot get stuck.
2 It may be wise to fix safety bars or good locks to windows.
3 Unnecessary falls can often be avoided by keeping toys picked up as much as possible.

Outdoors
1 Never leave your small grandchild in the yard on his own if you have a garden pond.
2 A good fence is a wise precaution.
3 See that the gate is latched.
4 Any side entrance and back gate should be well-secured, too.
5 Check that you do not have poisonous plants, shrubs, and trees in the garden.

The garage
1 All potentially dangerous equipment and liquids (gas, oil, paint, polish etc.) should be safely put away, and the car kept locked. If you have automatic garage doors, be sure the child cannot reach the operating mechanisms.

The shed
1 All garden tools should be kept locked away.
2 Keep all pesticides and weed killers locked away, too.

29

Traveling with children

Many children today are well traveled even before they start school. But getting about with children is in many ways an art. If a trip is to be relaxed and enjoyable, a certain amount of advance organization is necessary. Children did not travel as much twenty or so years ago, so you may never have spent much time traveling with young people. Luggage should be kept as light as possible and, since children like to be independent, a separate small suitcase may be appreciated. Favorite toys, coloring books, and games will keep children occupied on a long journey. Mugs that don't spill, moistened towelettes, tissues, and plastic bags will prove indispensable. But before you consider venturing off by train, air, or sea, you need to be confident about getting around with your grandchild at street level.

Just strolling

Check the brakes on any stroller or buggy that you use. Make sure that they are fully extended and locked into position, and use the safety harness, if one is provided. A sling is an ancient and convenient way of carrying a baby, leaving your hands free, but make sure that the infant is well secured and that he cannot fall out. Some slings are like a pouch, others are enclosed; but whichever you choose, support the baby's head whenever you lean forward. A backpack can be useful for a baby who can sit up well: but before investing in one, see if you will be comfortable wearing it. When out walking, a safety harness with reins will prevent your small grandchild from running into the road. It is important to teach older children the safe way of crossing the street at every opportunity.

Going shopping

If you and your grandchild go shopping together, whether to pick up the week's groceries or to a department store to choose clothes or a special gift, make the most of the occasion. Careful advance planning should make the shopping trip not only enjoyable for both of you but also something of a positive educational experience for the child.

Set out early to avoid the crowds and, if you are using public transportation, avoid the rush hours. It is no fun traveling with a child in a crowded bus. You may possibly need help getting on and off public transportation with a child. Don't be afraid to ask for assistance. Have your grandchild assist you with compiling your shopping list before you set off, and then he can help you find the items on the shelves. An older child can look at prices and special offers, and can become aware of the importance of good nutrition if you explain to him or her why you choose what your choose. Let them pay for purchases, too, and get them to check their change. If you are with a toddler, keep an eye open in case he or she picks items off the shelves, popping them into the shopping cart without your being aware of it! Either sit the toddler in the shopping cart if you are certain he will be safe and secure there, or have him on reins so that he will not wander off.

If you both dress in bright colors or something easily recognizable, you will be able to spot each other more easily if by chance you get separated. Make sure, too, once your grandchild is old enough to communicate clearly, that he or she understands exactly what to do if this does happen. Most important of all, never leave an infant unattended outside a store. And do not overload a buggy or stroller with shopping so that it is no longer safely balanced.

Children like to display their independence. You will see this often as a grandparent. But no youngster should be allowed to cross the street alone unless you are absolutely confident about his or her ability to cope with traffic. You will need to come to an understanding about conduct when crossing the street well in advance of an outing. You don't need to embarrass your eight-year-old grandchild by constantly holding his hand, but you should cross together. Sometimes children react positively if they feel they are helping an adult to cross. Managing two or more children on a shopping trip doesn't have to be that much more difficult if you give each of them a sense of responsibility for the other. Bring along a snack if you do not plan to stop to eat; children often find shopping a hungry business.

Eating out

On a short trip with toddlers, it is probably best to take along your own snacks: sandwiches or fruit, seedless grapes, raisins, or carrots, for instance. Fruit juices are preferable to fruit-flavored drinks, colas, and lemonade. A thermos will help to keep drinks cool. Picnics are perennial favorites with children. They don't have to be grand affairs: the picnic spot itself and the very fact that they are eating in a different environment altogether will be far more important to youngsters.

You may have to feed an infant grandchild when out. Disposable bottles with ready-to-use formula so that no washing or sterilizing are necessary are particularly useful. Or use an ordinary bottle, and take along hot water in a thermos either for mixing the formula or for heating the bottle. Never try to keep the bottle warm since this provides an excellent breeding ground for bacteria. Instead, heat up the bottle or mix the formula as required.

If you eat in a restaurant, choose carefully. Find one that is used to catering to young people. It may be a branch of one of the many chains that make eating virtually an entertainment for children if, of course, you enjoy that sort of food yourself! Other more traditional restaurants also often welcome children, providing highchairs and cushions, and even junior menus. Be wary of dishes that your grandchild has never tried before. To avoid the possibility of an upset stomach, hot food is better than cold. Peel all fruit and, if at all in doubt about the water, offer fruit juice or bottled water to drink. Don't eat or drink anything very hot while holding a small baby, for fear of spilling it and scalding him.

Out in the car

Traveling by car is the easiest way to get around with children, but it requires careful planning, especially for safety's sake.

If you take your grandchildren out fairly often, and you have a four-door car, you will need to check the safety locks are functioning. There are other precautions you must take, too. A portable crib or bassinet should always, and in many places by law, be carefully secured on the back seat. A toddler must be in a special safety seat, properly fastened to the body of the car, not just hooked into position. When a little bigger, he can be secured by a seat belt. Never let your grandchild travel either on his own in the front seat of the car or on your knee. This can be extremely dangerous.

Make an early start, if your car trip is to be a long one. Stop every hour or so to allow everyone time to stretch legs and to go to the bathroom, to get some fresh air and to enjoy a snack. It's better to stop to have something to eat rather than to do so while traveling. Let the kids change seats when you stop. This should keep them from becoming unduly restless too soon. Make it plain, at the first sign of any bad behavior, that it is simply not allowed in the car. Such disturbances can be annoying and highly dangerous for a driver. If, at any time, you feel yourself getting distraught because of their behavior, stop for a rest.

Magnetic games, a map or compass, I-spy contests, singalongs, and favorite stories on cassettes make excellent distractions on a long trip. Many of the games on pages 60-65 are suitable for playing in a car. Choose those that will not cause too much excitement. A blanket in the car is useful in case it gets chilly. Take along spare clothes in case of mishaps and some plastic bags, too, for litter or in case your grandchild gets carsick.

Avoiding travel sickness

Even though so many of today's children are experienced travelers, a number do become queasy or carsick at times. There are several things you can do to avoid this reaction, usually caused by the effect of motion on the delicate balance mechanism of the inner ear.

Make sure that your grandchild does not get too excited. He should also not have anything very rich to eat either before or during the journey. It will help to have either a window open or the airconditioning on, and to provide a nonsmoking environment. Reading may worsen the nausea. Don't repeatedly ask your grandchild how he or she feels but keep an eye open for warning signs. In case he is sick, have some paper bags, tissues, a moist cloth, and air freshener available, as well as something for him to suck on to take the taste away. If carsickness is a recurring problem, a doctor may recommend antiemetic pills. These often make a child sleepy, so don't be surprised if he nods off after taking them. It will help the journey pass more quickly and uneventfully for him. The tendency to carsickness, you will be relieved to hear if your grandchild is a sufferer, will probably disappear as he gets older.

By air, sea, and train

Any long journey will go more smoothly if you disturb a child's normal sleep patterns as little as possible. Avoid lengthy waiting periods by consulting timetables carefully in order to achieve the best connections possible. A good travel agent should be able to advise you as to the best routes when traveling with a child.

If you're going by air, advise the airline in advance that you will have a child with you. Most airlines will provide amusements by way of books, games, or toys and will also help with warming a baby bottle and other small chores. Most airlines board passengers with children first, which will make things easier for you and be less confusing to your grandchild. If they are available, try to reserve bulkhead seats. They will allow you far more space when traveling with a toddler.

Traveling with children

A nonsmoking area is preferable, too. If the airline does not provide stroller, you may be able to take along an umbrella stroller as handluggage. When traveling with a small baby, you may find a sling particularly convenient. Arrive at the airport well on time, and bring along in your in-flight bag small toys or games to amuse your grandchild when you take off and land. If this is to be the first time your grandchild has flown, quell any nervousness by promoting the journey as an adventure. Explain in advance about the noise at takeoff and landing as this often comes as something of a shock to small children. Allow a small child to stretch his legs from time to time when the aisle is free. Unless there is really annoying behavior, most passengers would probably rather be disturbed for a few moments this way than to suffer the whining of a miserable toddler for hours on end. Make allowances for moods, too, once you arrive. It takes time not only to adapt to a new environment and perhaps to a different climate, but also to a new time zone. The same will of course be true for the return journey which you make.

Although few children in this country have the opportunity of traveling on a train, you could find yourself traveling with a grandchild across country or using the excellent trains that run in Europe and provide inexpensive transport.

Children may want to stretch their legs on a long train journey, but it isn't safe to allow them to wander along a corridor on their own. Window seats are best, because children enjoy the view, but see they play fair with one another and change seats every now and then. Most children love traveling by train and since there is often a great deal of excitement, you will want to see that those sitting nearby are not bothered by small children. Bring along plenty of books, games, puzzles, and drawing materials to keep them amused. If windows can be opened, your grandchild should be warned about the dangers of leaning out.

An ocean voyage or cruise can be an extremely pleasurable, if somewhat rare way of traveling with children. Some liners have special facilities for the young. But a choppy crossing on a small craft may be very uncomfortable for the child with a tendency to travel sickness, and thus not too pleasant for you either. For children who have found their sea legs, however, a journey by boat can be the most enormous fun. Be sure that they understand the ship's safety rules and know how to use safety equipment.

Happy holidays!

If your grandchild's parents are not able to take a family holiday for some reason, you might want to take the children on vacation with you. Toddlers are probably happiest at home: but once a child is a little more self-confident, he may find the idea of going away with you very appealing.

Traveling by car is an easy way to get around with toddlers. Note that a special seat will be absolutely essential.

Holidays abroad are a great adventure. Tell your grandchild all you can in advance about the country you are visiting.

32

Traveling with children

A holiday in a rented house or apartment will allow plenty of freedom as far as entertainment and cuisine are concerned. If you are an experienced camper, a holiday under canvas with your grandchildren could be a tremendous adventure for you all, too. Some campgrounds have play areas, laundromats and baby care facilities but you need to do some homework first to check up on the availability of such services. Choose a site with good entertainment nearby, in case the weather lets you down. But if you are hoping for more of a rest, you may prefer to opt for a hotel so that meals and services are provided. Look for a hotel that caters to children. They will probably be able to offer babysitting, early meals, laundry service, and perhaps a gamesroom so that children can be kept amused if the weather is bad.

Farm holidays are favorites with children from an urban environment. They will be fascinated by such activities as milking and haymaking, and they may even be allowed to help with certain farm duties – feeding the chickens, for instance – as well as to watch. On fruit farms, they may be able to join in with the picking if the season is right.

If you choose a beach resort, and it is the first time that your grandchild has been to the ocean, he or she may be a little frightened of it at first. A sandy beach is preferable and you will have to watch him constantly. On no account should a child be in the water on his own, nor should he be allowed out alone on a raft or inner tube, or in a paddle-boat or small craft of any kind. A large number of accidents occur by the sea simply as a result of negligence. All children who cannot swim should be wearing life jackets or at least water-wings or a rubber-ring, even if paddling.

Protect your grandchild's sensitive skin from the effects of too much sun. Children tend to burn easily. A sun hat is useful, as is a sunshade or umbrella, and a canopy for a buggy. Cotton clothes in light colors are best. Use a sun cream with a high protective factor, reapplying it regularly. Restrict his exposure to five minutes the first day, increasing it by five minutes per day. It is easy to burn especially when in the sea or a swimming pool. Sunburn can be very painful, particularly for a toddler. Remember, too, that in the heat, your grandchild will be perspiring more than usual, and so will require more to drink.

If your grandchild does get mild sunburn, the best thing is to apply calamine lotion. This will have a soothing effect. Dress him in something soft and keep him out of the sun for a while, since this will only aggravate any discomfort. If a really bad sunburn occurs, your grandchild is probably in a lot of pain and a doctor should be consulted. As always, prevention is preferable to cure, so do everything you can to see that the holiday is not ruined for your grandchild because of excessive exposure to the sun.

In case of small accidents, it's a good idea to take with you a basic first aid kit containing suntan cream (with a high protective factor for fair skin), a soothing lotion for sunburn, scissors, tweezers, bandages, cotton tipped swabs, antiseptic cream, insect sting reliever spray, and a packet of needles (to be sterilized before use) for removing splinters and thorns. Ask your doctor whether it would be wise to take along any other items for your particular destination. Take out adequate travel insurance for everyone on the holiday in case of illness, accident or loss of luggage. Unexpected medical bills on top of holiday expenses can make quite a hole in your budget and you will feel more relaxed if you know that you are insured.

Food when abroad

If you are unsure about the sort of food that will be available for an infant while you are away, it would be wise to bring along a few favorite canned foods. But if these are not finished at one meal, do not try to keep them until the next, particularly if the weather is hot since the food is likely to go off easily. Similarly, try to avoid foods you suspect may be reheated when choosing from a menu, since there is greater risk of food poisoning with these. Introduce any older grandchild very gently to foods which are rather highly spiced or in any way very different from those that he or she is used to eating at home, because these may be rejected. Children are very conservative as far as food is concerned. You may like to take along some medicine recommended by your doctor as suitable for children, in case of stomach upsets.

Family holidays

It could be, of course, that you might be invited to join your grandchild's family on a holiday. Be prepared: you may be asked to help with baby-sitting on several occasions, not only at night but possibly also during the day. This will be fine on the whole: but it may be a good idea to come to an understanding about this if you would like some time to yourself during the vacation.

It is generally advisable to book any holiday with you grandchildren as early as you can, so that you will have as much choice as possible by way of location, as well as suitable accommodation and facilities.

Find out well in advance if any immunizations are necessary if you are traveling abroad and see that your grandchild has a valid passport. Phrase books and maps of the locality will add a further dimension to the holiday, making the whole expedition an adventure for the participants.

Children and pets

It is very often a grandparent who buys a child his or her first pet: a small puppy or kitten, perhaps, or a guinea pig or canary. A child can gain enormously from learning to care for a pet. Not only will he come to appreciate all that is involved in feeding and cleaning up after an animal or bird and so, in turn, what is involved when adults look after him, but he should also gain better control of his own emotions as he exerts a certain amount of control over his pet's behavior. The desire to be loved, and to love, is quite intense in a child: and he will find that, no matter how he has behaved, it is a very great comfort to believe that his dog or his hamster still cares. This is a very common source of reassurance to a child.

Most child psychologists would agree that for a child to have a pet is probably a very good thing in principle. There are, however, certain factors you ought definitely to take into account before you set out for the pet shop. First and foremost, you should find out if your grandchild's parents would welcome a pet in the house. Some adults simply do not like having certain animals in a domestic situation. Others may be concerned about being out at work all day long and leaving a pet alone. Some might be worried about the additional expense of feeding a cat or a dog if the household budget is already tight. Others might feel strongly that a child is not yet old enough to look after the pet properly on a daily basis. It may not be a good idea either to have a dog with a new baby in the house. Sometimes a pet is also contraindicated because of allergies. A family consultation is really necessary, even if you plan for the pet to be something of a surprise. It would be disastrous to buy a pet for your grandchild and then to have to return it to the breeder.

You will also have to consider the size of any pet in relation to your grandchild and his environment. An Alsation puppy may be quite small at first, but he will not be easy to handle in an apartment when he is a full-size dog. You will also need to provide a basket, hutch, or cage for the pet. Make sure that your grandchild is prepared to take a puppy for a walk regularly, to feed him, assist in training him, or to feed and play with a kitten or other pet. You might want to arrange for your grandchild to attend a special course in dog handling: or to provide some of the accessories necessary for pet care – a lead, brush, a basket, toys or a specially engraved name tag, for example.

Pets and health

Certain diseases can be caught from pets. If you are buying a bird, check that a parrot or budgerigar, for instance, has been vaccinated against *psittacosis*. This is a fairly rare condition, but if caught from a bird, it can result in pneumonia. You will also need to see that a dog or cat is dewormed, and that any fleas are eradicated. Sometimes, too, a skin rash may result from an allergic reaction to a pet's hair or fur. The possibility of a bite from a pet is always something of a risk, particularly if it is teased, so warn your grandchild about this. If it does happen, the prinicpal risk will be tetanus. See the doctor right away. He will want to know if the tetanus immunization is up to date and he may decide to give a booster shot. Very serious diseases, such as rabies, hardly ever occur in countries where there are strict quarantine laws. So if your grandchild goes abroad, you will have to explain why his pet cannot go along, too; and why, perhaps, you will be looking after his cat or dog. Encourage your grandchild to see that his pet is examined by a veterinarian at regular intervals, and whenever sick. Explain to him why he shouldn't eat his pet's food or give to his pet food other than what is recommended. Teach him not to touch the animal's feces, never to kiss a pet near its nose or mouth, and always to be sure to wash his hands after playing with the pet and certainly before touching any food.

Other pets

If space is at a premium, or your grandchild is not fond of cats or dogs, you may prefer to get him a fish bowl or an aquarium. You can start with just a couple of colorful fish and add to the tank from time to time as a surprise. Be sure that your grandchild fully understands the perils of overfeeding. You can buy him a manual, written especially for children, that will explain all the intricacies of looking after an aquarium. A turtle, too, can make a delightful pet. More affluent grandparents might think in terms of a pony, but upkeep can be extremely expensive, and it could be absolutely heartbreaking for a child if his parents had to sell his pony for financial reasons. On a more modest scale, tadpoles can be bred as pets, and so can ladybirds and caterpillars, at least for a while.

Children and pets

Pets can be enormous fun. But will your grandchild's parents welcome a rabbit or a puppy?

A pet can be a wonderful companion for an only child: while in larger families, a child may have to learn to share the responsibility of looking after an animal, or to have the care of one to himself.

The nervous child

If you have a grandchild who is patently scared of animals, you could perhaps take it upon yourself to help him or her over this difficulty. Most children take to animals quite instinctively, but an unfortunate experience can frighten a toddler. Dogs that jump up and bark a lot, even small ones that yelp and yap, can easily startle a child. Start by introducing him to a small and very docile breed of dog. Choose one that is used to children. Let him pat the dog, and permit a mutual trust to develop. He may want to clutch your hand or hide behind you at first, but confidence will soon develop. Bear in mind, too, that if *you* have a dog who is devoted to you, it may display signs of jealousy if your small grandchild comes to stay. Because dogs sometimes resent all the attention given to small babies, you may want to keep them apart for a while until they get used to each other. Never leave them alone together, and always have a net in order to protect your grandchild in his buggy when out in the yard.

If a pet dies

Your grandchild's first experience of death is likely to be that of a pet. Parents often refuse to buy a pet simply because they want to avoid the upset its death may cause a child. The greatest mistake you could make, and unfortunately one made only too often by grandparents, is to replace the pet at once. So don't rush to the nearest pet shop to find a similar breed in the attempt to help your grandchild forget. In his eyes, there really could never be another Willoughby, Scrap, or Joey. He needs time to mourn his pet and even perhaps to hold a funeral.

It is wrong for an adult to hide the dead pet from the child, or to bury it secretly. Instead, give your grandchild a while to grieve, and wait for him to ask for another pet that he will in turn care for and love just as wholeheartedly, whether it be a similar breed of cat or dog or a different animal altogether. Just as your grandchild may learn about the inevitability of death from a pet, so if his cat has kittens, for example, he may become aware of the whole process of procreation, another valuable experience.

Outings and treats

There will be many occasions when you want to take your grandchild on an outing, perhaps to give his parents a little time to themselves, perhaps during school holidays, or perhaps because you know you will enjoy the day, too! Outings don't have to be lavish occasions. To be successful, they simply require a little forethought and planning.

Museums and galleries

If the very word 'museum' conjures up for you a picture of a stuffy, forbidding old building, housing boring relics from a bygone age, you have probably not been in a gallery of this kind lately. There have been so many changes in museum presentations and displays that you are in for a surprise, and the chances are you will enjoy the visit quite as much as your grandchild does.

A museum visit is perhaps inadvisable for three-year-olds and under, although some children's museums cater to even very young children. Most major cities have a science museum, often with working models that can be operated by twisting knobs and pressing buttons. There may even be a lunar module to examine. A natural history museum may house a vast dinosaur, as well as other species long since extinct. Museums such as these often provide special activities for children: animal noises to listen to, for instance, hands-on exhibits, souvenirs, and educational publications. Toy museums are enchanting to adults and children alike. Transport, maritime, and local history museums can also provide many an entertaining afternoon. Art galleries now often offer special holiday programs and organize competitions for children. Even children of five and six enjoy looking at paintings and sculpture, will have quite definite likes and dislikes, and can talk about them quite coherently. A planetarium will, of course, fascinate the child interested in stars and space travel.

Around and about

A child should get to know something about the area he lives in: its history, its layout and architecture, its industry, and its population. Depending on where you live, you may find that there are special sightseeing tours. These may usually be for foreign visitors but can also be enjoyed by children, once they are old enough to follow a guide's commentary. Do check, however, that such tours are not too long. A child's concentration span is far more limited than that of most adults. Half-a-day's sightseeing will be more than ample for a seven or eight-year-old.

You can organize your own sightseeing tours, too, taking in all the principal buildings and using a map together. Some factories, newspapers, toy manufacturers, car assembly plants, and food industries also offer tours to the public. County and state fairs are another source of entertainment and learning. If you have a major waterway in the vicinity, you might also enjoy a river trip, perhaps taking along a picnic lunch. The country-dwelling child will naturally particularly enjoy a visit to the big city; for him, it will count as a great adventure.

Parks and playgrounds

Most cities have a certain amount of open space within their boundaries, and many parks and playgrounds offer specific recreational facilities. Some stage children's shows or puppet plays during the summer, or have carnivals from time to time or a permanent amusement park. Before you take your grandchild on any ride, however, be sure that he or she is comfortable with the idea and understands what will happen on the ride. A fearful reaction can be difficult to handle. Then, too, *you* may not like the idea of a rollercoaster ride, and a small child should not go unaccompanied, however hard he nags you.

The circus and the zoo

Most children love animals; and for them, there could be no greater treat than a visit to a zoo. Some have a special children's corner or petting zoo, providing an opportunity for toddlers to meet farm animals face to face. For even greater excitement, visit a safari park, where animals are in more natural surroundings. Be sure that your grandchild understands all the park rules and regulations. It will usually be a sensible precaution to keep the car windows closed.

The circus, which may feature many animal acts, as well as highwire performers, magicians, acrobats, and clowns, is a fantastic form of entertainment for children. You might like to check on the reputation of the circus that you are considering visiting in order to see whether animals are trained with kindness, however.

Outings and treats

A day in the country

The city child will usually find a day in the country exciting, especially if you plan the outing well in advance, perhaps by introducing a special theme. You might, for instance, spend an afternoon with a field guide, trying to identify wild flowers. Don't allow your grandchild to pick any, however, as some may be rare species. Instead, get him or her to write notes about the plants you find, and perhaps to sketch them, too. Starting an illustrated nature diary in this way can be a fascinating activity.

Identifying different trees can also be fun, and your grandchild will enjoy collecting their leaves and fruit. Look for birds' and squirrels' nests, and for insects, too. Measure the growth of a really big tree and if you find the stump of a tree that has been cut down, assess its age by counting the number of annual rings. Take home some ripe seeds – acorns, perhaps – and show your grandchild how to grow his own seedlings. First soak the acorn overnight in warm water. Peel off the outer shell, if possible. Find a pot, and place some stones at the bottom of it, in order to help the water drain well. Put soil or compost into the pot, and water the soil so that it is moist. Place the acorn on top of the soil, and cover it with another layer. Fasten a plastic bag over the pot to keep the acorn moist without further watering. Then place the pot in a sunny spot. When you see signs of a seedling in a few weeks, take off the bag. Water it just once or twice a week. You can either leave it in the pot for a while or replant the seedling oak in the ground as an excellent memento of a day in the country.

See that your grandchild is suitably dressed for a day out of this kind.

A day on the beach

Choose a fine day for an outing to the ocean or to a lake. Nothing can be more frustrating for a child than to see the water and not be able to run on the sand or to wade. Be prepared for a baby or toddler to be just a little frightened at first. The water may be cold and he may not like its wetness. The sound of the ocean is also sometimes scary for very young ears. You will need all the usual paraphernalia: buckets, spades, water toys, beach towels, shady hats, sun lotion, and a change of clothes. Watch out for sunburn as a child's skin is very tender. Spend very little time out in direct sun. Remember to keep reapplying sun lotion as it will get washed off in the water. Don't allow your grandchild in the water on his own, or without you keeping constant watch. Rafts can be dangerous, and have been known to result in disastrous accidents. Consider carefully the safety aspects of all water activity before you let your grandchild join in water play of any kind. Bring plenty to drink, and keep it cool in a thermos. This will be greatly appreciated on a hot day, and far less costly than buying drinks on the spot. Take along a first aid kit, too, just in case of mishaps.

Stage and screen

Most city guidebooks include a section devoted to children's entertainment, and you will probably find many activities available for three-year-olds and over, including puppet and magic shows, plays, films and concerts. Some are presented by traveling groups who set up tents in parks. Certain community projects feature programs specifically designed to appeal to those who might otherwise never visit a theater and sometimes their repertoires will include plays suitable for children. Some have regular Saturday morning performances especially for children and many even involve the kids themselves in drama workshops. A movie outing can be enjoyable but check on the rating of the film first, to see that it really is suitable for your grandchild's age group. Why not consider renting a VCR and some films, too. Many orchestras give performances especially for children, and this often provides an excellent opportunity to introduce them to the various instruments. Public libraries and local elementary schools also often have programs for youngsters.

Sports of all sorts

The child who loves sport will find it a very special treat to be taken to a game of some kind. Try to get the best seats you can so that he or she has a really good view of the game. You may tend to feel that such an outing is perhaps pointless if the match can be viewed at home. But an outing of this kind should prove to you that there is no comparison between seeing a live game and being part of the action and watching sport on television.

If you once enjoyed certain sports actively yourself, you may like to take your grandchild along, perhaps to a junior judo or karate class, to skating or skiing lessons, to tennis, to basketball or to the swimming pool (but again, do not allow him in the water alone unless a skilled swimmer).

An outing with a grandparent can be an enormous treat for a child. But in many respects there is something more to be said for it than that. It also marks a step towards his independence, because you have a rather different role from that of a parent. Your grandchild will probably find it exciting telling everyone all about the day's activities and, if all has gone smoothly, which it should have with good planning, you will both be looking forward to the next occasion when, for a treat, you go out for the day together.

Fun in the yard

By introducing your grandchild to the delights of your yard at an early age, you will be fostering an active interest in natural history as well as an appreciation of the importance of conservation. The bright colors and alluring scent of such plants as sunflowers, nasturtiums, roses, and cornflowers are only part of the enjoyment a love of the outdoors can bring. Once you start looking at your yard from this new angle, you will probably be amazed at how much wildlife there is there, no matter how far you are from fields and woodlands.

Birds and butterflies

Consider building a bird feeder in the yard and providing seeds, nuts, and water for winged visitors, especially in winter when their natural food is scarce. Watching birds feeding in this way will not only provide a child with great entertainment but also increase his knowledge and understanding of natural history. Tell your grandchild not to disturb any nests he finds in hedges or trees, and to leave any eggs to hatch.

Children love butterflies, too, so do everything you can do to attract them to your garden. Wild plants like ragwort, nettles, and fleabane are all favored by butterflies, as is *buddleia davidii*, which is sometimes called the 'butterfly bush'. Watch for the common monarch butterflies, the tiger swallowtail, red admirals, and skippers, as well as rarer varieties, on warm summer days. Nearly all children are fascinated by the transformation from caterpillar to butterfly. In general, the wilder and more overgrown a yard, the greater its potential butterfly population.

Pond and animal life

If you have a pond, your grandchild's safety will be your first concern. But this doesn't mean that your grandchild can't be introduced by you to the wealth of wildlife to be found in water. You can introduce frog or toad spawn into the pond: any

However small the yard, there are still many ways you will be able to introduce your grandchild to the delights of gardening. A plot of his or her own is bound to be very welcome. Those without a yard, meanwhile, will be able to grow plants in hanging baskets, window boxes or tubs. There are many possibilities for play out of doors, too.

Fun in the yard

child will be fascinated by the metamorphosis of these creatures.

Watch together for interesting insects, dragonflies and beetles, for instance. Even something as seemingly ordinary as a swarm of ants can provide intriguing viewing. Warn the child, however, to be wary of snakes or swarming bees and to tell you at once if he spots them. Your yard may also play host to a number of other visitors: squirrels, voles and mice, for instance. Encourage your grandchild to look for these creatures, but not to disturb them unnecessarily. You can also leave food for them.

Playing in the yard

A yard, in a child's eyes, is not only an area for growing flowers, shrubs, and perhaps vegetables, but a play area, too. If you are a conscientious gardener, proud of your flowerbeds, rockeries, and lawn, you will have to see that any such activity area is situated well away from prized plants, and that ball games are played at a distance from the house, garage, or greenhouse. Remember, too, that constant activity may soon cause bare patches on a previously smooth lawn. So you might want to provide your grandchild with his own special play area. Even a comparatively small yard can have a play corner of this kind. A spot somewhere near the house is particularly suitable while your grandchild is still a toddler, so you can keep an eye on him. While children are small, they require careful supervision when at play.

A sandbox is always a great favorite with small children, and provides an opportunity for imaginative play. You can either buy one ready-made or make your own by filling an old rubber tire or plastic wading pool with silver sand, which will not stain in the same way that ordinary building sand will. Cover the sandbox when it is not being used, or it will attract stray cats and dogs.

Children love playing both in and with water. If you provide a wading pool for summer afternoons, it will be particularly welcome. A garden hose can provide a great deal of fun on a really hot day, too. But carefully supervise any infant or toddler when there is water around, no matter how shallow it is, and even if he can swim. An enormous number of accidents occur in water.

Many indoor toys can be brought outdoors in summer, but some are for the yard only. Jungle gyms and swingsets are major purchases that encourage physical coordination: but not all good outdoor toys have to be that expensive. A tree swing can be simple to make, but you must be sure that it is secure and that a small child cannot fall out. A couple of lawn chairs draped with old curtains or sheets make an excellent playhouse or tent for a toddler. Exploit wooden planks, ropes, and ladders for an adventure playground area for older children. They will also enjoy the wilder parts of the yard, which may provide great hiding places. A treehouse is, of course, something many children hanker after, but you will need to be quite fit in order to get up there yourself to build one.

Fun in the yard

Letting your grandchild have a plot of his or her very own in your garden in which to grow flowers is a wonderful idea. For a very small investment on your part in a few packets of seeds, he will have a great deal of pleasure. Choose plants that flower quickly. Children are impatient by nature, and like to see the results of their efforts without too much delay. You will want to select brightly colored plants, and perhaps those with a marked fragrance. Try to see that his plot always has something interesting growing in it. You might help your grandchild plant seeds so that the final display will spell his name. Visit a garden center together to select plants. And make sure that he is responsible for tending his own patch of garden, and that you are not expected to do all the work. It is important for children to learn that if benefits are to be reaped, they have to be worked for, and gardening is an excellent medium for conveying this philosophy. Having his own set of junior gardening tools should prove an added incentive.

The vegetable plot

Many children enjoy growing vegetables even more than flowers. They will even proudly contribute their own produce to a meal, otherwise tending to refuse vegetables! A homegrown product *does* taste better. Let them choose which vegetables to plant, and guide them carefully in the use of compost and fertilizers. Most important of all, let them pick what they have grown. Potatoes, cabbage, peas, beans, cucumbers, and tomatoes are particularly popular. A children's gardening book will make a good present for the real enthusiast. Encourage your grandchild to label plants and to keep a gardening diary, noting what needs doing when. Even if you live in town, it may still be possible for you to introduce a child to the delights of homegrown produce but on a smaller scale, perhaps by growing herbs indoors (a very quick process) or tomatoes in pots in a sunny place. Your grandchild will certainly benefit. It is amazing how many children living in towns have no idea how potatoes, beans or cucumbers grow.

Your grandchildren will also enjoy helping you harvest fruit, but warn them about eating unwashed produce or indulging too much while picking, which may bring on stomach upsets. Rhubarb, while an excellent fruit, does have poisonous leaves, so point this out to your grandchild if you grow the plant.

Garden ornaments

While children are still of an age when they enjoy stories about fairies, they will be delighted by any stone or plaster gnomes and pixies with which you decorate the garden. Adults may look down on them as crude, but children adore them, just as they do other garden ornaments such as sundials, statues, and scarecrows. Making a scarecrow together can be a wonderfully amusing occupation. Save old clothes and hats for this purpose, and use straw to stuff the body.

See how they grow

Not until your grandchild is a toddler will he or she be able to enjoy planting seeds and bulbs, tending them, and seeing them grow and flower. But even before then, the very birth of your grandchild can be celebrated in the garden, by the planting of a tree to commemorate the occasion. This can then become his or her very own tree, of exactly the same age. A small tree like a birch or crab apple, for instance, a magnolia or lilac bush may be particularly suitable. Your grandchild will also be able to measure his growth against it year by year.

Of all garden plants, sunflowers appeal to children perhaps the most. Their rate of growth in a single season is tremendous, some reaching ten feet or more, and your grandchildren might even like to compete to see whose sunflower grows highest. Another plant in which children commonly delight is the snapdragon. Show your grandchildren how its mouth can be made to open if they press gently at the sides of the flower, and they will soon see how it gets its name. Flowers that open in the early morning and close in the afternoon, the California poppy and morning glory, for example, are also a source of great fascination for children. But not only cultivated plants will be of interest. Many so-called weeds will be fun for your grandchildren to play with, too. A lawn on which there are daisies will provide for a small child the means of making decorative chains with these wild flowers, while the new generation will still probably enjoy blowing dandelion seed heads to the wind.

Legends and tales

Enjoy telling your grandchildren how many of our flowers got their names. The daisy, for instance, is so called because it used to be thought that it resembled the 'day's eye'. In the morning, its petals open, just like an eye; in the evening, they close, as if in sleep. Legends about plants abound. One story, for instance, tells how a princess once saw some lovely blue flowers by a stream. She asked a gallant young prince to pick some for her. He went to do so but, alas, fell into the stream. With the flowers in his hand, and sinking since he could not swim, he earnestly cried out "Forget-me-not", which is how the plant got its name. With a little research, you should be able to unearth some enchanting tales and folk lore about common plants and flowers. Names like fairy thimbles, cathedral bells, and red-hot poker are fascinating to young children. Play games together with daisies, picking the petals until you find, according to the word of the rhyme which accompanies the last petal, whether marriage will be to tinker, tailor, soldier, sailor, beggarman, or thief; whether this year, next year, some time, or never; or whether in silk, in satin, in cotton or rags.

Pressed and dried flowers

Your grandchildren may enjoy the ancient craft of flower pressing, too. Pick a variety of flowers when they are at their best and on a dry day. Carry them carefully and press them as soon as you can, under a heavy weight, for a few weeks. No special equipment is required – a few books will do – but you can buy or make a proper flower press for this function. The best flowers for pressing are small and fine: primroses, buttercups, violets, roses, marigolds, and daisies are especially suitable. You can avoid unnecessary loss of color by drying the petals and leaves as much as possible as soon as they are picked. Yellow and orange flowers tend to keep their colors well, whereas red flowers fade more easily. Grasses, ferns and leaves also press well. Pressed plants can be made into pictures or used to decorate album covers, candles, tablemats, bookmarks, or greeting cards and gift tags. A potpourri or lavendar bag can also be made from dried flowers, and children love helping you make these from the plants they have picked. See that the flowers are in prime condition, and picked after the dew has dried. All that is needed is a cool, airy, dry, dark place. Tie them up in small bunches, and see that the heads are not too crowded. Hang the plants upside down so that the flowers will keep their shape and the stems remain straight. Most plants will dry in about a week, but some larger ones may take longer. The dried flowers can then be displayed in all sorts of decorative ways, and will not require water. They will be an excellent reminder of the times you spend in the garden together. But do remind your grandchild not to pick rare species of wild flowers, and explain why.

Poisonous plants

Berries, mushrooms, and flowers are very attractive to small children, so you must do everything you can to prevent a toddler from eating them as a number of garden plants can be highly poisonous. Lily of the valley, for example, which grows wild but is also commonly cultivated, can cause severe abdominal pain, an irregular pulse, and coma. Bluebell bulbs can cause diarrhea and stomach cramps. Foxglove leaves (*digitalis*) are used in medicine for their action on the heart but if eaten in quantity may cause irritation of the stomach and even stop the heart. Ivy leaves and berries, yew berries, and deadly nightshade can cause severe poisoning in small children, as may laburnum tree bark, leaves, and flowers, while the common field buttercup may cause dermatitis in those who are particularly sensitive.

If you suspect that a child has eaten the berries, bark, leaves, or flowers of these or any other plants – mushrooms and toadstools, too – you should immediately take him or her either to your nearest poison center or to the nearest emergency room, bringing a sample of the plant with you, if possible. Meanwhile, take from his mouth any bits he has not swallowed, and make him sick by putting two fingers to the back of his throat. But don't make him vomit in this way when lying down or he might choke. See that he is upright when you do this, and keep him calm.

The alternative garden

Even if you have a very small yard, you may still be able to grow flowers with your grandchild in hanging baskets, tubs, or troughs. You can also have fun together growing indoor plants. You might choose, for instance, to plant some bulbs together, to put aside as a springtime or Mother's Day surprise. You can assure your grandchild that you will tend any indoor plants that he or she leaves with you. You may also prepare cuttings for him to take home. Busy Lizzies (*Impatiens wallerana*), spider plants (*Chlorophytum comosum*), ferns, sweetheart vines (*Philodendron scandens*), Swiss cheese plants (*Monstera deliciosa*), rubber plants, and the Venus flytrap are often popular, and so is mother-in-law's tongue (*Sansevieria trifasciata*), if you will forgive its name. Plant a hyacinth bulb in water in a wide-necked jar and your grandchild will be able to watch not only the leaves and flowers grow, but also the roots. Make sure that your grandchild takes caring for his or her indoor plants seriously. You could perhaps provide a basic handbook about indoor gardening and a guide to actual plants with their Latin and more common names.

If your grandchild has no yard at all at home – perhaps he and his parents live in a small apartment – his visits to your yard will be all the more appreciated. But even if his parents have a yard, there is still something rather special about having a plot of one's own elsewhere. There is something rather special, too, about the young and the old working together with nature in this way. As you spend time together, you will also be cultivating a relationship between you and your grandchild.

Things to make

Many enjoyable hours can be spent not only making things *for* your grandchildren but *with* them, too. Even if you have never regarded yourself as particularly handy, you should still find it fun making simple toys, often using common household items, things you might normally throw away. From now on, start looking at cardboard boxes, paper towel rolls, and egg cartons in a new light! With a little imagination, you can make an amazing variety of playthings in just an hour or so. The projects that follow should provide some ideas for you to develop, using your own original designs.

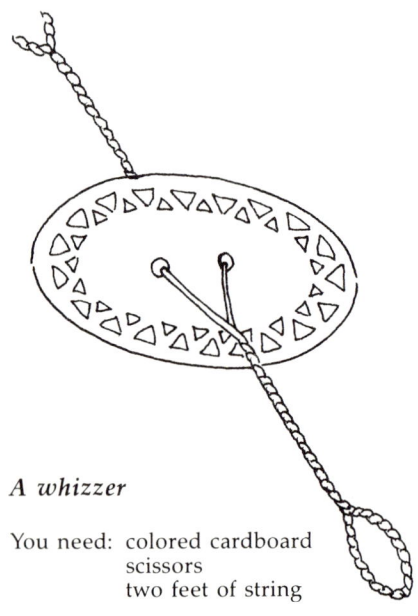

A whizzer

You need: colored cardboard
scissors
two feet of string

Cut out a circle from the cardboard. You can make a border decoration with further cutouts, if you wish. Make two holes towards the center of the card, and thread a piece of string through one hole back into the other. Tie the ends together. Spin the disc until the string is wound up, then pull the string.

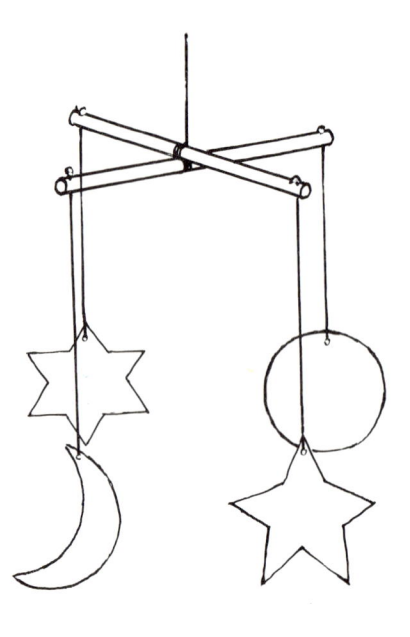

A mobile

You need: colored cardboard
scissors
thread
pipe cleaners

Join two pipe cleaners at the center by twisting them together so they form an x-shape. Cut out four different shapes from the colored cardboard. Make a hole in each decorative shape and run a piece of thread through it, tying the ends of the thread to a branch of the pipe cleaner holder. Then tie some thread to the center of the holder and attach the mobile to the ceiling. This is a delightful toy to hang over a crib.

English egg cozies

You need: colored felt
needle and thread
paper and pencil
scissors

Make a boiled egg more inviting by providing an amusing cover for it. Sketch the basic outline to use as a pattern. Then cut out two identical shapes in felt, and sew them together leaving a sufficiently large opening for placing over an average-sized hen's egg. Decorate according to the design you have in mind.

Advent calendar

You need: two sheets of plain cardboard
utility knife
paints and brushes
glue

Paint a large Christmas tree shape on one of the sheets of cardboard. Cut out twenty-five flaps by marking and cutting three sides of a square for each flap and scoring along the fourth side. Paint a number on each flap. Then glue the other piece of cardboard to the back of the first. When the glue has dried, open each flap and paint a small picture in each. Explain to your grandchild that the first surprise 'door' is to be opened on the first day of December, and another door every day.

Things to make

A sampler

An excellent way of marking the birth of a grandchild is to make a sampler to commemorate the occasion. You can create your own design for this, drawing it in advance on graph paper, and deciding beforehand on the color scheme. Traditionally, a sampler of this kind is worked on canvas and features the name of the baby, his or her date of birth, perhaps the names of his or her parents, and a combination of cross-stitch and floral designs that can also be used to form a decorative border. Either frame the sampler yourself, or have this professionally done.

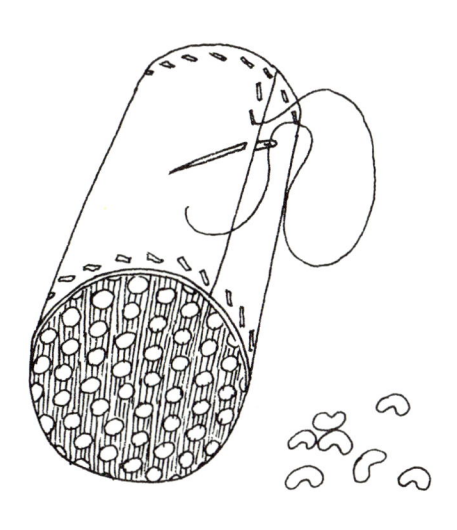

A baby's rattle

You need: a small cardboard tube or a hair curler
needle and thread
dried beans
scissors
small piece of fairly thick, washable fabric and some lining

Cut out the fabric and lining, making sure that they are large enough to fit around the cardboard tube, with allowance for seams. Cut out circular pieces for the ends, again leaving a seam allowance. Sew the covering for the tube, remembering to leave one end open to insert the dried beans. The ends will need to be well sealed.

Christmas pillows

You need: old pillowcases
needle and thread
remnants of fabric

Instead of hanging the traditional Christmas stocking, some families prefer to have pillowcases. Using odd bits of fabric, decorate old pillow cases with a Christmas collage: a picture of a Christmas tree, Santa Claus, or an angel, perhaps.

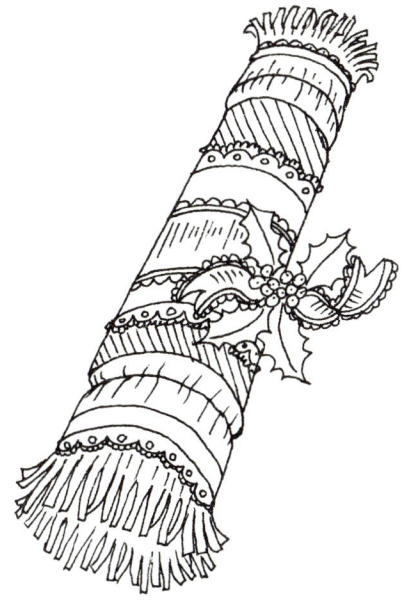

Party crackers

You need: crepe paper
small gifts
mottoes or jokes
paper hats
cellophane tape
ribbon
aluminum foil
scissors
decorative string
small cardboard tubes

For each cracker, take two tubes. Cut one in half. Inside the uncut tube, put a present, a paper hat, and a motto or joke. You may also be able to obtain special strips that will make a noise when the cracker is pulled. If you have managed to get hold of these, put one next to the filled tube on top of a piece of foil and a longer piece of crepe paper. Place the two shorter tubes at either end of the larger tube, leaving a small gap between each. Roll up the two layers of paper and fasten with cellophane tape. Tie two pieces of decorative string between the tubes. Decorate the outside of the cracker with ribbon, and use scissors to make fringed ends.

A chorus line

You need: a long sheet of paper
paints and brushes or crayons
scissors

Fold the paper accordion-style into several equal panels. Draw an outline of a figure on the top panel and let the hands meet the edges of the paper. Cut out the figure and open the panels. The figures will be holding hands in a row. Now color and decorate each figure.

Paper chains

You need: colored construction paper
paste
scissors

Cut out strips, each about 6 inches long and ½ inch wide. Form the first strip into a ring and paste down one edge as it slightly overlaps the other. Continue to do this, linking one ring inside the other, until you have a chain of the length required.

43

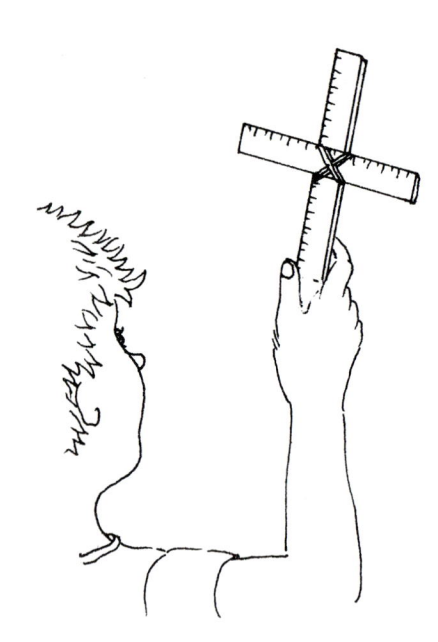

Things to make

Special message card

You need: paper
scissors
felt pens

Fold the paper in half vertically. Make a small horizontal cut in the spine about a third of the way from the top. Open the card. Score a small diamond shape around the cut. Fold the card horizontally. Put a finger into the cut. Fold along the scored lines. Write a special message inside the opening diamond shape. Making this the 'mouth' of an animal or bird, draw the creature on the inside of the card, and decorate the front of the card.

legs to the back of the puppet with the fasteners. Tie a piece of the string or thread between the arm pins and also between the leg pins. Then join a piece of string or thread from the middle of the string joining the arms to that joining the legs, and leave an end hanging. When you pull the string, the limbs move.

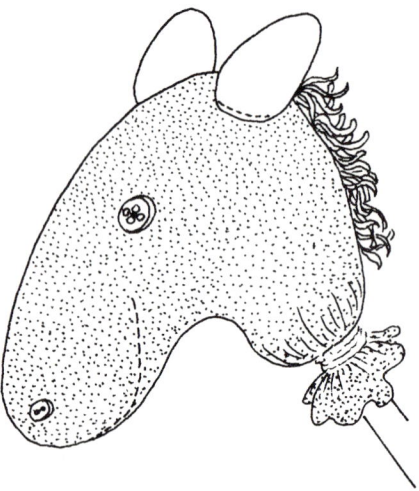

Hobby horse

You need: a clean broom
a piece of fabric
strands of yarn
two large buttons
one smaller button
string
rubber bands
needle and thread

Cover the brush of the broom with a piece of fabric. Make the ears by gathering the fabric with rubber bands or yarn at two corners. Sew on the two large buttons for the eyes, and use the smaller one to suggest a nose. Use yarn to make a mane.

A boomerang

You need: two strips of wood, each about 12 inches long
thread and a thick needle
instrument for making a hole

Make certain the ends and corners of the pieces of wood are sanded down. They should look like two rulers, each having a slightly curved long side. Make a hole in the center of each. Place the pieces of wood across one another to form a right angle. Tie them firmly together with the thread through the holes. When throwing and catching the boomerang, wear a glove. Throw the boomerang only outdoors. Instruct your grandchild to throw the boomerang by holding the bottom of one of the pieces of wood in one hand so that the thumb is along the edge nearest to him. He should have his arm raised behind his shoulder about level with his nose, and should face the wind. Then he should swing and throw the boomerang to the right, if it is in his right hand. It will take a great deal of practice and patience before he can get it to come back. There can be no guarantee it will work: but there will be a lot of entertainment for everyone.

Jumping teddy

You need: cardboard
paints and brushes
or crayons
scissors
paper fasteners (or clasps from old manilla envelopes)
thin string or thread

Draw an outline of a teddy bear's head and body on the cardboard, but draw his arms and legs separately. Color in the outline, drawing in facial features. Cut out the teddy's head and body, and separate arms and legs. Join the arms and

A teaching clock

You need: colored cardboard
scissors
felt tips
paper fastener
compass
pencil

Use the compass to draw a large circle on the cardboard (or draw around a large saucepan). Draw a slightly smaller circle within this. Using felt tips, mark the clock figures in the usual

44

Things to make

positions. Cut out around the larger circle. Now make two clock hands, one smaller than the other, from another piece of cardboard. Make each hand from a different color of cardboard. Fix the two hands to the center of the circle with a paper fastener. Make sure that the hands can be moved easily.

A flicker book

You need: about 20 sheets of paper
stapler and staples
scissors
pencil or felt pen

See that all the pieces of paper are the same size. Staple them together. Draw a character in the center of the first page and on each page that follows (best of all, towards one corner). Draw the same character in various stages of some activity, such as dancing or throwing a ball. Flick through the book. The character you have drawn will seem to move, just as in a cartoon.

Floor cushions

Large floor cushions are often more appealing to children than are chairs. You could make one as a special surprise, and personalize it with an appliqué initial.

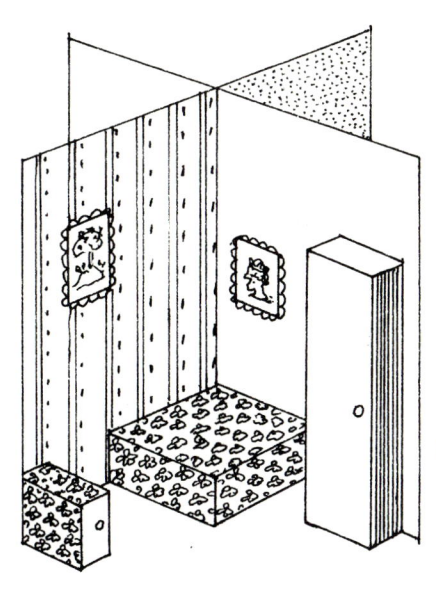

A miniature house

You need: three large squares of thick cardboard
scissors
glue or tape
scraps of wallpaper
wallpaper paste
postage stamps
matchboxes

A dollhouse doesn't have to be elaborate. Take two of the squares of cardboard and cut slits half way through the middle of each. Slide one slit into the other. Stick these two pieces – the walls of the house – to the third piece of cardboard, which will be the floor. You now have a dollhouse with four rooms. Decorate with scraps of wallpaper and knit carpets or rugs. Make one room a kitchen, one a bedroom, one a dining room, and one a living room. Old postage stamps can be used as pictures on the wall, and painted matchboxes turned into pieces of furniture.

Patchwork

Once your grandchild knows how to knit, you could perhaps both contribute towards a knitted patchwork bedspread for him or her by making six-inch squares in a variety of colors. Sew these together for a beautiful handmade bedspread. Remnants of fabric are also useful for patchwork items of all kinds, so do save them. Tiny scraps can be used for a doll's patchwork quilt.

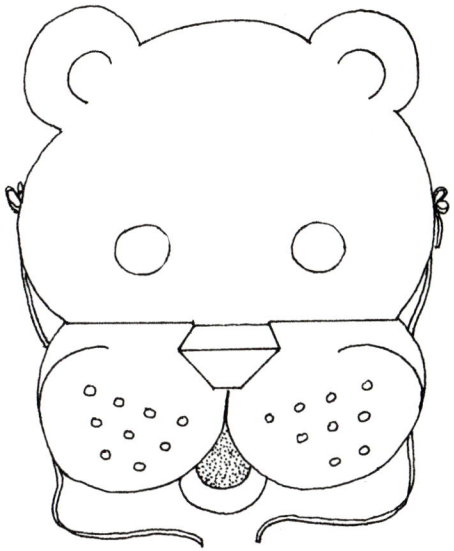

Papier-mâché masks

You need: a mixing bowl
wooden spoon
two tablespoons flour
one pint hot water
cake pan
vaseline
newspaper strips
scissors
paint brush

Mix the flour and hot water to make a thick paste. Cover the inside of the cake pan with the vaseline. Soak the newspaper strips in the paste for a few moments. Press each strip to the pan so that it hangs over the edge. The whole pan should be covered. Do this in several layers, with the strips always overlapping. Put on more paste and smooth the paper mold. Leave for forty-eight hours. Remove the paper shape. Trim the edges with scissors. Bind with more strips of paper soaked in paste. Decorate with facial features according to the effect required. Make holes for eyes, nose, and mouth, and pierce holes for a fastening to be tied around the head.

45

Things to make

Lace cut-outs

You need: a large sheet of paper
scissors

Fold the paper in half several times. Cut out triangles and various shapes in the folded paper. Then open it. You will have a decorative lace-patterned piece of paper which might be used as a plate cover or doily.

A crystal garden

You need: a glass jar or tank
water-glass (a solution of sodium or potassium silicate)
crystals of copper sulphate, iron sulphate, alum and any other crystals suggested by a pharmacist
quartz (white) sand
a knitting needle

Pour warm water into the jar until it is about half full. Add the water-glass and stir it in. Add the sand so that it is about one inch deep. Put in the crystals one by one, and poke them into the sand with the knitting needle. In a few days, the crystals will start to grow as colored strands. Note: this 'scientific' garden is suitable only for older children and the chemicals used should only be bought and handled carefully by a responsible adult.

Play dough

You need: 1 cup salt
1½ cups flour
½ cup water
2 tablespoons of cooking oil
food color

This dough can be used to make a variety of things; for example, beads, to be strung on yarn after they have air-dried (use a toothpick to shape the holes). If stored in a plastic bag or container in the refrigerator, the play dough will keep well.

A castle

You need: pieces of thin colored cardboard
cellophane tape
scissors

Draw on the cardboard the elongated shape of a round tower. Cut out the shape, so that the battlements stand out. Cut out the door, too. Roll the tower into a cylinder and tape it. To make the conical towers, roll over the corner of a piece of cardboard until it makes a point. Then tape the cone and cut off the excess cardboard. Roll a smaller piece of cardboard into a tube and tape it. Fix the cone on top. Use cardboard to form the castle walls. Decorate with flags that can be fastened with tape.

Birthday card

You need: 1 large piece of thin cardboard
scissors
paints and brushes or felt pens

Fold the card lengthwise into twice the number of figures you will require. Draw half the shape of the figure you choose, a clown, perhaps, and cut out the shape with the card folded. The middle of your figure must be at the fold. If you make a slight angle at the bottom, the row of figures will stand better. Color the figures carefully, and write your birthday greeting on the back. Cards which children have made themselves are always greatly appreciated.

French knitting

You need: an empty wooden spool
a hammer and four nails
a short knitting needle
yarn

Hammer four nails, evenly spaced, into the top of a wooden spool. Thread the wool through the center of the spool and wind it around each nail. Then use the knitting needle to pull the yarns over the nails. The cord that is made this way will come through the hole in the reel. You will need to finish off the cord with a knot in order to stop it from unraveling.

Things to make

Dollhouse furniture

You need: empty matchboxes
glue
tape
corks
cardboard
remnants of fabric
scissors
aluminum foil
paints and brushes
or felt tips
buttons

A chest of drawers is easily made by gluing together three painted matchboxes, one on top of the other. Buttons can be used for handles. A bed can be made from the inside of a matchbox, with four small pieces of cork for legs. Use remnants of fabric for bed covers. Living room, kitchen, and bathroom furniture can be made in much the same way, using straightforward household items.

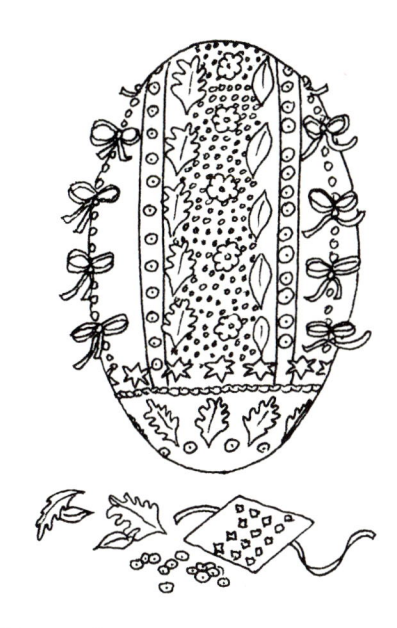

Decorative eggs

You need: eggs
a pin
enamel paint or nailpolish
water
tinsel, foil, beads
glue
gummed stars (optional)

Remove the inside of the eggs, since they are not to be eaten. This is a tricky job, calling for careful handling. Make a hole with the pin at one end of the egg. Make a larger hole at the other end. Try to break through to the yolk. Take a bowl and blow into the small hole. Shake the egg gently if the contents get stuck. When you think all the yolk and white are out, let a small stream of water into the larger hole, and then blow out the water. Dry the shell, and decorate the egg with either enamel paint or nailpolish. Felt tips are also suitable. Decide on your design before you start to paint. Or decorate the egg by painting it first and then applying scraps of tinsel, foil, beads, and stars, all of which can be glued on.

Jigsaw puzzle

You need: a large sheet of cardboard
a large picture, cut out from a magazine
scissors
paste and a brush

Stick the picture onto the cardboard. Wait until it dries. Trim the cardboard. Cut up the picture into a variety of shapes. To make a double-sided jigsaw (more of a challenge to complete), paste another picture on the back of the card before you cut out the pieces. For an even more complex jigsaw, pick particularly busy pictures and make more intricate pieces.

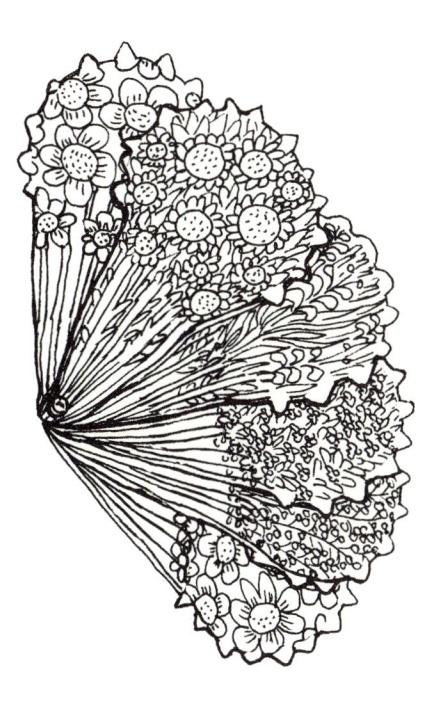

A fan

You need: thin cardboard
crayons or felt tips
scissors
tape or needle and thread

There are several ways of making a fan. One simple method is to cut out a basic fan shape with a point at the bottom, sides that widen, and a rounded top. This can then be decorated with any picture or design. When the card is dry, it can be pleated. The end to be held should be bound with tape. Or, using thicker cardboard, cut out a number of identical elongated shapes and decorate them. Make a small hole at the bottom of each shape and then join them together with thread.

Potato prints

You need: several large potatoes
a knife
poster paint
paper or cardboard

Cut a potato in half, and then cut away, from one half, any parts you do not wish to paint – that is, the design you wish to print should be raised. Dip the potato half into some paint, and then press it onto the paper or cardboard.

47

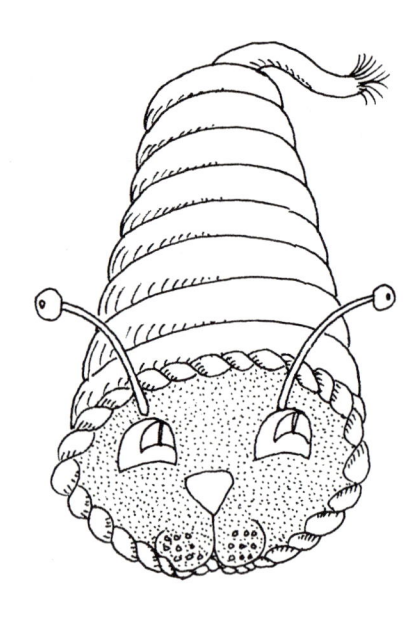

Things to make

Badges

You need: air-drying clay
cardboard
scissors
glue
brooch fastenings
knife
paint
varnish

Roll out the self-hardening clay to the desired thickness. While you let it harden, draw on the cardboard the shapes of the badges you want to make, and cut them out. Place them on the clay, and cut around them with a knife. Let the basic badge shapes dry for at least twenty-four hours. Then paint them, and allow to dry. Varnish and again allow to dry. Glue on the brooch fastenings.

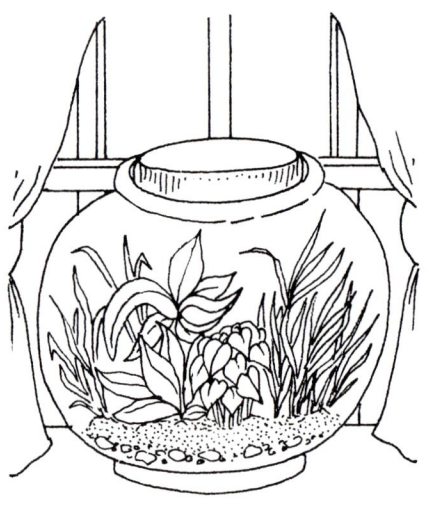

firmly. Pour about a half cup of water through the funnel into the soil. Put on the cork lid, and place the bottle garden by a window but not in strong sunlight. Open the lid for a few hours every three weeks or so. If the plants grow too large, prune them.

A caterpillar

You need: a cardboard tube
scissors
green fabric
beads or buttons
needle and thread
yarn

Either cover the cardboard tube with fabric or wind yarn around it. Cut out circles in the fabric for the two ends. Make an allowance for seams. Use beads or buttons for facial features, and perhaps decorate the fantasy caterpillar with strands of wool.

Puppet theater

You need: a cardboard box
a few long sticks
large pieces of cardboard
paints and brushes
scissors
tape

Cut off the top and bottom flaps of a large rectangular cardboard box. Cut a rectangle out of the front, too. Make various backdrops by painting scenes on a number of pieces of cardboard that can be taped to sticks and lowered into the box. Children can give a performance in the theater by balancing the box between two chairs on top of a long piece of cloth hanging to the floor. They can hide behind the cloth and work hand or finger puppets from below.

A bottle garden

You need: a wide-necked glass jar and cork lid
some pebbles
garden peat and potting compost
a few small plants
a funnel
water

Place a few pebbles at the bottom of the glass jar. Mix the garden peat and compost. Put the soil into the jar and press it down. Makes holes for the plants and press them in

A shell frame

You need: a wooden picture frame
various shells
glue
varnish
large sheet of paper

Clean the shells and let them drain on absorbent paper. Sketch on a large sheet of paper exactly how you will arrange the shells. Glue each shell to the frame in the position selected. Paint with a layer of varnish when complete. Select a favorite photograph to display in the frame.

Musical water jars

You need: six or more different sized jars or bottles
pencils, for use as beaters
labels

Label the jars, each with a different number. Fill each with a different amount of water. The jar that has most water in it will have the lowest note. Experiment

Things to make

for sound by tapping each glass with a pencil. You should be able to produce a recognizable tune. Alter the water levels as necessary.

A raffia dolly

You need: strands of raffia
needle and thread or yarn
scissors
remnants of fabric
buttons

Take twelve pieces of raffia about 10 inches long, fold them in half, and bind them with thread about ½ inch from the fold. This will form the head. Taking up the two bundles of twelve pieces of raffia, tie each bundle near the bottom. Take six more strands of raffia, and pass them through the body. Cut to a reasonable length for the arms, and tie at the wrists. Tie the arms to the body so that they stay in position. Use fabric to make a face, and buttons for the features. Make clothes for the raffia dolly, too, from left-over scraps of fabric, or knit some tiny garments.

Rose perfume

You need: scented rose petals
water
two small bottles with a cork or screwtop

Put as many petals as possible into the bottle and fill it with water. Put on the bottletop. Set aside for two or three days. If there is now more water needed, fill up the bottle and replace the top. After two or three weeks, pour the water into the other bottle. You should find you have some delightfully perfumed rose-water which your grandchild might like to give to his or her mother as a gift.

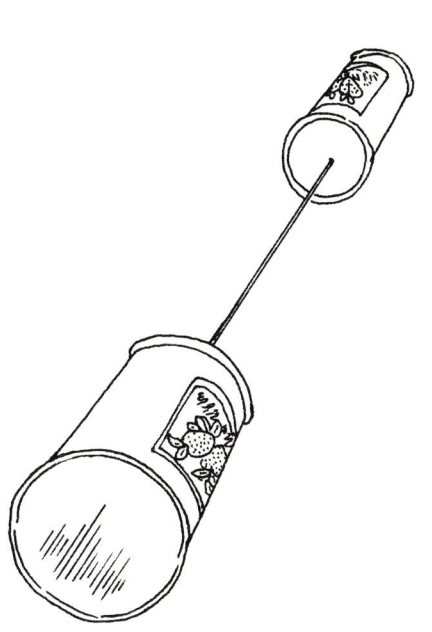

A jungle telegraph

You need: two empty cans with each end removed (check that there are no dangerous sharp edges)
string

Make a hole in each can and join them together with the string, knotting each end. If you stretch the string so that it is taut, you should be able to hear a message whispered into one can, if you hold the other to your ear. This makes an great secret-agent game.

Shadow puppets

You need: a white sheet, a large piece of white cardboard, or a plain white wall
scissors
cardboard and wire
a strong light

You can use either cardboard cutouts fastened onto wire or your hands to portray various animals and characters. If using a sheet, stand behind it with the light source correctly positioned so that the shadow falls onto the sheet and can be seen by the audience in front of it.

You and your grandchildren can either stage a show based on a well-known story, or you could make one up.

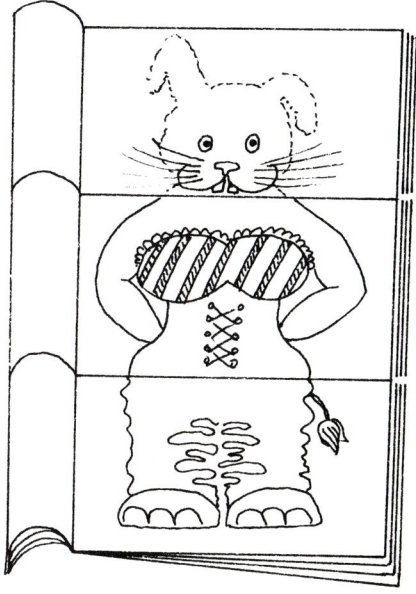

Crazy characters

You need: several sheets of paper
a ruler
a pencil
paints and a brush
 or felt pens
scissors
a stapler

Fold the sheets of paper, which should be of equal size, and staple them so that they form a book. Fold back the cover and, using the ruler, divide each page horizontally into three. Draw a different figure on each page, the body in the central section, and the legs in the bottom third. Then cut each page along the ruled pencil lines. The more varied your characters, the more fun you can have when you turn the different sections of the pages to make some really crazy characters!

Things to make

A town plan

Children aged six to ten should find it an entertaining challenge to make a map of their town. It doesn't have to be drawn to scale, but could simply show the position of such buildings and areas as their house or apartment, school, park, police station, hospital, shopping center, bus stops, and any major monuments. Compass directions should be marked in, too.

Dressing-up

A great many old household items can be adapted to make a whole wardrobe of dressing-up clothes. Save old drapes, tablecloths, and bedspreads, handbags and hats, wigs and hair pieces, shirts and pajamas, even shoes. Your grandchildren will love having a box full of dressing-up clothes. Net curtains can be made up into a bridal gown, old sheets can be sewn to make a nurse's outfit, pajamas to make a clown costume, and a discarded felt hat reshaped in a variety of styles.

Baubles and beads

Most small children will love threading beads to make a necklace or bracelet. Beads don't have to be expensive and, attractive pieces of jewelry can even be made from dried beans, which can either be left a natural color or colored with nontoxic paint. But don't let a baby play with beads as they are easily swallowed and could cause choking.

Blow paintings

You need: straws
paint
paper

Make sure that the table is well protected. Make some pools of watery paint on the paper, and get your grandchild to blow at the paint through a straw. He should find he can make some fascinating abstract patterns in this way.

Finger puppets

You need: colored felt
small beads or buttons
needle and thread
colored yarn

Make tubes of felt that fit your fingers. Sew on small beads or buttons for the eyes and nose, and yarn for the hair and mouth.

Bird feeder

All that is needed is a piece of wood, suitably treated for outdoor use and approximately 15 inches square, fixed to a post about 5 feet from the ground. A strip of wood about 1 inch deep should be attached to the edges, but leave a gap at one corner for drainage. Set out bread, nuts, fat, and other scraps for the birds.

Collages

There are so many things you can use for a collage. Supply your grandchild with some of the following: fabric, toothpicks, leaves, shells, buttons, pieces of wallpaper, yarn, string, popsicle sticks, dried flowers, pebbles, bottle caps, even macaroni. He can draw his picture and then assemble the collage.

Christmas tree decorations

A tree, brightly lit, laden with presents and colorful trimmings is one of the excitements of Christmas. Here are some ideas for *edible* decorations.

Icicles and pinwheels

1/4 cup soft margarine
4 tablespoons lemon juice
1½ lbs confectioners' sugar
red, green, and yellow food coloring
thread

Melt the margarine and lemon juice in a saucepan over a low heat. Do not boil. Sift in 8 oz of the sugar and reheat slowly to allow the sugar to dissolve. When the mixture bubbles, cook for two minutes only. Remove the pan from the heat and sift in another 8 oz sugar. Beat until cool enough to handle. Turn onto a board, sprinkle with the remaining sugar, and knead until smooth. The more it is kneaded, the whiter the icing will be. Cut off one third of the icing. For icicles, use half of the third. Make a hole with a skewer for the hanging thread. Lay on a tray and put in a warm place for the icing to firm up. For pinwheels, divide the remaining two thirds into three, and color each differently. Roll out the remaining white icing to a rectangle approximately 8 inches x 5 inches. Place on one side. Roll out the colored icings to the same size and lay one on top of the other. Place these on the white icing. Roll up like a jelly roll to about 2 inches x 8 inches. Trim the ends and cut into thin slices. Allow to dry like the icicles.

Corkie canes

Makes 24
3/8 cup butter or margarine
3/8 cup sugar
3/4 cup flour
1½ level tablespoons cocoa powder
½ level teaspoon baking powder
1 small egg
1 package of jelly beans
tinsel cord or ribbon

Preheat the oven to 375°F. Cream the butter or margarine and sugar together until light and fluffy. Sift flour, cocoa, and baking powder together. Beat the egg and add to the creamed mixture, beating well. Stir in the sifted ingredients. Knead the mixture together to give a fairly stiff dough. Place the dough on a lightly floured surface and divide into 24 pieces. Shape into lengths of about 6 inches. Curve one end for the handle. Place on a lightly greased baking sheet. Cut the jelly beans into half pieces and press them into the dough. Bake for 10–12 minutes. Leave for a few minutes before removing to a cooling rack. When cool, tie a bow or length of tinsel around the handle of each so they are ready to use as decorations.

Things to make

Snowballs

¾ cup sifted confectioners' sugar
½ cup flaked coconut
3–4 tablespoons sweetened condensed milk
cord or thread

Place the sugar in a bowl. Stir in ¾ of the coconut. Add 3 tablespoons of the condensed milk and knead the mixture together. Add extra milk if necessary to get the mixture together. Turn onto a clean work surface and continue to knead until fairly smooth. Divide the mixture into 30 pieces and make into balls. Keep them in a plastic bag after making so they will not dry out. Cut the thread into 4-inch lengths and tie the ends together. Place the remaining coconut on a sheet of waxed paper. Knead each ball until smooth, make a hole with a skewer, and put in a loop of the knotted cord. Knead again to enclose the cord and roll each ball in the coconut. Place on a tray and leave to harden.

Snowpeople

Makes 6
½ cup margarine
¼ cup sugar
vanilla extract
½ cup flour
1 oz cocoa
Icing
1½ cups confectioners' sugar, sifted
Decoration
12 currants or raisins
2 or 3 candied cherries
chocolate candies
4 chocolate cookies

Cream the margarine and sugar together. Add a few drops of vanilla extract, then sift in the flour and cocoa and mix well. Divide a third of the mixture into six pieces and divide the remaining dough also into six pieces. Roll all the pieces into balls. Place the smaller balls about ½ inch above the larger ones on a greased baking tray, spaced fairly well apart. Leave in the refrigerator to chill for about ½ hour. Bake in a moderately hot oven (375°F) for 12-15 minutes. The head and body should join during baking. Place carefully on a rack to cool. Mix the sifted confectioners' sugar with a little boiling water to form a fairly stiff frosting. Using a teaspoon, cover each snowman shape with frosting and, while still wet, press on a face made with the raisins and cherries. Cut up the chocolate cookies and use pieces to make top hats. Place two chocolate candies down the center of each and leave to dry.

Marzipan animals

You need: marzipan
food color
nonpareils and colored sprinkles
small paper containers

Place a little of the marzipan in a bowl, and add a drop or two of food coloring. Roll the marzipan into a ball, and divide into sections. Then form into different animal shapes, using different food coloring. Use the nonpareils and sprinkles to decorate. Place in the small paper containers.

There is great fun to be had with grandchildren prior to Christmas making edible decorations, such as the snowpeople panorama shown here. But do remember to supervise very carefully when it comes to using sharp kitchen implements and a hot oven. The recipes for icicles and pinwheels, snowballs and corkie canes are well worth trying, too.

Bon appetit!

'What is the matter with Mary Jane?
She's perfectly well and she hasn't a pain,
And it's lovely rice pudding for dinner again,
What is the matter with Mary Jane?'
                               A.A. Milne, Rice Pudding

There is nothing more disconcerting for whoever is cooking than to prepare a meal and find that it is not well received or that only half of it is eaten. You may be convinced that roast beef is an excellent dish: but if a child has developed a dislike for meat, you will have little success in tempting him with a plate of it. Katherine Whitehorn, writing in *How to Survive Children*, gets to the essence of it all, reminding the reader that a food is not necessarily essential just because a child hates it.

So don't force your grandchild to eat what he does not find enjoyable. Your meals together are far more likely to be successful if you cook with both good nutrition and your grandchild's favorite foods in mind. That is not to say that you must change your normal daily menu entirely. But you could easily introduce an element of compromise by presenting your grandchild's portion of the family meal in a particularly attractive way. Even the very names you give your dishes can affect your grandchild's reaction to them. Call a recipe by some entertaining title, and the chances are this will not only amuse him but also, as a result, please his palate all the more.

Cooking for grandchildren inevitably requires advance planning. For many years now, the contents of your cupboards and refrigerator may have served for excellent adult meals, even to gourmet standards perhaps. But meals that most children favor, you will find, are rather different. Fads and fancies need to be taken into account, too. First find out whether your grandchild has any particular likes or dislikes.

Making mealtime an adventure will definitely pay dividends for the child who is a rather finicky eater. On the pages that follow you will find many ideas for presenting wholesome dishes in a number of unusual and attractive ways.

When feeding an infant grandchild who is just beginning to eat solid foods, you should closely follow the list of foods his parents are giving him. For three-year-olds and over, however, you can be more ambitious. Cooking for your grandchild can and should be fun, but bear in mind certain health and safety suggestions.

- Do not serve fish to an infant or child without first carefully removing the bones.
- Use as many fresh, unprocessed foods as possible.
- Do not serve packaged or frozen foods after the expiration date.
- Avoid unnecessary use of salt.
- Do not cook a frozen chicken until fully thawed, which may take as long as twenty-four hours.
- Never leave a baby alone when he is eating.
- Frozen foods are more nutritious than canned and sometimes more so than supposedly fresh merchandise that may have been on display in the store for too long.
- Watch for signs of possible food allergy: a rash, a stomach upset, sickness, or a headache. Foods most commonly linked with allergy include cows' milk, additives, citrus fruits, chocolate, and eggs.
- Don't force your grandchild to eat what he does not want.
- It is probably not a good idea for a toddler or child to drink more than one pint of milk per day.
- Wholewheat cereals, wholemeal bread, and wholewheat pasta are far better for your grandchild than white, refined foods.
- Avoid offering food or sweets as a reward.
- Give as few sweets as possible between meals. They will only destroy a healthy appetite, and in the long run may promote tooth decay.
- Fruit juice is preferable to fruit drinks, colas, and other soft drinks, which should only be given occasionally.
- Do not worry if your grandchild dislikes meat. Cheese, eggs, baked beans, and fish also contain protein.
- Keep all hot food and drinks away from a baby's reach to avoid scalding.
- Wash all fruits and vegetables under running cold water to remove both dirt and chemicals.
- Do not give a small grandchild whole nuts; toddlers can easily choke on them.
- Avoid highly spiced dishes until your grandchild is older and serve this sort of food only if he is used to it.

Bon appetit!

A hearty breakfast

Breakfast is considered by nutritionists to be an important meal for everyone, and particularly for children. It should set them up for the day, so that they are not too tempted to fill up on sweets and snacks before lunch. For a great many families, however, it tends to be a hurried affair. So why not make breakfast something more special when you prepare it for your grandchildren? You might choose to cook a full English-style breakfast, with bacon and eggs, and perhaps fried bread and sausages, too, or to go for visual impact by livening up a simple but nourishing boiled egg by painting its shell. The traditional Dutch breakfast of cold meats and cheese is also an appealing one. In summer, a mixed fruit salad can be both refreshing and delicious. Toast cut into fingers and topped with peanut butter, or homemade Swiss-style granola, garnished with fruit, are full of valuable nutrients, too. Below, are some other ideas for you to try.

Hot apple muffins

Makes 20–24 muffins
1 cup flour
1 level teaspoon salt
3 level teaspoons baking powder
¼ cup sugar
2 eggs
½ cup milk
¼ cup melted butter
½ cup peeled and chopped apples
Topping (optional)
4 medium-sized red dessert apples
5 tablespoons sugar
1 tablespoon ground cinnamon

Grease 24 two-inch muffin tins and pre-heat the oven to 425°F. (If using the topping, prepare it by coring and peeling the apples and cutting each into 4 or 5 thick rings. Mix the sugar and cinnamon together and coat the apple rings.) Sift dry ingredients in a mixing bowl. In another bowl, beat the eggs and then add the milk and melted butter. Stir the liquid very quickly into the flour mixture. Fold in the chopped apples. Fill the greased tins one-third full. (If topping, put one cinnamon apple ring on each muffin.) Bake for 15 – 20 minutes.

Granola

Serves 4
¾ cup rolled oats
¼ cup raisins
Grated rind and juice of one lemon
2 cups milk
2 bananas

Mix all dry ingredients together with the lemon juice. Add milk. Cover and leave in a cool place overnight. Serve topped with sliced banana.

Gone bananas!

Serves 1
½ teaspoon honey
1 carton natural yogurt
1 banana
5 tablespoons rolled oats
1 tablespoon raisins

Mix four tablespoons of rolled oats with the yogurt and honey. Peel and slice the banana. Add half the banana slices and the raisins to the yogurt mixture and pour into a dish. Sprinkle the remaining oats onto a piece of foil, and toast until golden brown. Sprinkle the toasted oats on top of the banana and yogurt mixture. Decorate with the remaining slices of banana.

Checkerboard breakfast

Serves 1
1 large slice of bread
tomato sauce
2 oz each of two differently colored cheeses
1 slice ham

Toast the bread under the broiler on one side only. Spread the other side with the tomato sauce and place the ham on top. Cut both cheeses into cubes. Place them on top of the ham, alternating cubes, leaving a little space between each one. Place under broiler until the cheese begins to melt.

Drinks to delight

For thirsty grandchildren, try a variety of nutritious and delicious drinks.

Strawberry pink

Serves 2
4 tablespoons vanilla ice cream
1 small carton strawberries
1½ cups milk

Put the fruit, and two tablespoons of juice if canned or frozen strawberries are used, into a mixing bowl. Save two strawberries for decoration. Add the ice cream and the milk. Whisk until blended.

Bedtime story

Serves 1
2 oz dark chocolate
¾ cup milk
1 egg

Break the chocolate into pieces and put into a saucepan with the milk. Melt the chocolate gently in the milk, stirring constantly with a wooden spoon. Remove from the heat. Separate the egg yolk from the white. Add the egg yolk to the saucepan and mix thoroughly. Whisk the egg white in a mixing bowl until stiff. Add to the hot milk mixture and whisk.

Honey and lemon soother

Serves 3
1 tablespoon honey
1 tablespoon lemon juice
1½ cups milk
1 cup evaporated milk

Whisk all the milk together in a mixing bowl. Add the honey and mix well. Heat gently in a saucepan. Add the lemon juice.

Fruit cup

For each drink:
orange juice
soda
grenadine
slice of orange

In a tall glass, mix equal parts of chilled, fresh orange juice and soda. Add a splash of grenadine. Place a slice of orange on the rim of the glass.

Bon appetit!

Lunch and dinner

You should have no problem getting your grandchildren to eat with the recipes that follow. The way you present food is very important as far as young people are concerned. Even the names of some of the dishes suggested below will add excitement to mealtimes. Some, we anticipate, will soon become favorites. Remember that curries and other very spicy dishes may not be readily welcomed unless a child's palate is already accustomed to them. Keep portions to a reasonable size. They can always ask for more! Fresh foods are always preferable but you will find it useful at times to have so-called 'convenience' foods as a standby. Frozen foods are, incidentally, often more nutritious than those that are canned. Their vitamin content in particular is usually higher. Look carefully at the defrosting instructions. Hamburgers and other 'fast' foods can form the basis of a well balanced, highly nutritious main meal.

Potato faces

Serves 4
1½ lb potatoes, mashed with milk and butter
6 sausages
4 small tomatoes
7 oz can sweetcorn
4 slices cucumber, quartered
4 sprigs parsley

While the potatoes are cooking, grill the sausages and tomatoes, and heat the sweetcorn. Make potato faces on four dinner plates by spreading the potato over the base of the plate. Use a sausage to make the mouth, half a sausage for the nose, halved tomatoes for the eyes, sweetcorn for the hair and a bow tie for additional decoration from the quartered cucumber and sprigs of parsley.

Hamburger kebabs

Serves 4
4 frozen hamburgers
6 slices of bacon
4 tomatoes, quartered
½ cup uncooked rice
½ cup frozen peas
4 skewers

Cut the frozen hamburgers into quarters and cut each rasher of bacon into two and roll up. Arrange a piece of hamburger, tomato, and bacon roll on a skewer, alternating them until you have used 4 pieces of hamburger on each skewer. Cook the rice and peas. Cook the kebabs under a moderately hot broiler, turning occasionally, for eight minutes. Serve on a bed of rice and peas. Remove the skewers before eating. Serve with a favorite relish, sauce, or pickle.

Sausage ships

Makes 8
1½ lb potatoes, peeled
8 sausages
3 tablespoons butter
3 tablespoons milk
4 oz grated cheese
salt and pepper
8 slices processed cheese
baked beans
8 toothpicks or sandwich flags
(Note: take care that children do not swallow the sticks)

Boil the potatoes and cook the sausages. Drain the potatoes and mash with the butter, milk, and cheese. Season. Place into a piping bag with a large star nozzle. Cut the sausages almost

Potato faces are fun and also highly nutritious

Try these potato pets the recipe for which is on page 56.

54

Bon appetit!

Supper is plain sailing with these scrumptious sausage ships.

Bring potatoes to life with the Jaws recipe overleaf.

in half lengthwise and open out. Pipe the potato on top, and grill until golden brown. Cut each slice of cheese into two triangles. Sandwich a cocktail stick in the center of each triangle to form a sail. Place one on each sausage. Serve on a sea of baked beans for a visually exciting meal that most young children will love.

Beef and bean bonanza
Serves 4
1 tablespoon oil
1 large onion, chopped
½ cup sliced mushrooms
15½ oz baked beans
4 hamburgers, cooked and cut into pieces
3 thin slices bread, buttered
4 oz grated cheese

Heat the oil in a large saucepan and gently fry the onions and mushrooms until soft. Add the baked beans and hamburger pieces and simmer until heated thoroughly. Now pour into a shallow 2-pint ovenproof dish. Cut the bread slices into triangles and overlap on top, buttered side up. Sprinkle with some grated cheese. Place under the broiler until the cheese melts and bubbles.

Hot dog castle
Serves 4–6
¾ cup mashed potato
1 cup frozen peas
frankfurters
2 carrots, cooked and sliced into several pieces
1 slice ham
toothpicks
savory cheese sticks
(Note: take care that children do not swallow the toothpicks)

Prepare mashed potatoes and keep hot. Cook the peas and keep hot. After cooking the hot dogs, cut one-third off each one, and then cut each one-third in half. In the center of a large ovenproof plate, shape a square of mashed potatoes approximately 4 inches x 4 inches. Place the large hot dog pieces at each corner, pressing them into the potatoes to hold in position. Use most of the remaining pieces of hot dog to form battlements on top of the potatoes and wedge a piece of sliced carrot between. Press the savory cheese sticks vertically around the potato castle walls at intervals. Arrange the rest of the hot dogs in the center of one side of the square to form a drawbridge and cover with savory sticks. Make four flags using the toothpicks as masts and the ham as flags, and stick these into the four corners of the castle. Surround the castle with peas to form a moat. If the castle needs reheating, place in an oven pre-heated to 350°F for approximately 15 minutes.

Halloween hamburgers
Serves 8
2 large cooking apples
8 hamburgers
8 tablespoons grated cheese
8 buns
mustard or tomato ketchup

Grill one side of the hamburgers, and turn them. Put an apple ring on top of each hamburger and grill until golden brown. Cover with the grated cheese and put back under the grill until the cheese has melted. Split the buns and spread lightly with mustard or tomato ketchup. Fill with the apple-topped hamburgers and serve in colorful paper napkins. This is a substantial and warming snack for youngsters, who – supervised – could enjoy cooking the hamburgers for themselves.

Bon appetit!

Vegetable variations

It is sometimes difficult to get children to eat vegetables. But they are an important part of a balanced diet, and are best eaten when raw whenever possible. Vegetables don't have to be boring, as you will see from the ideas that follow. A crisp, fresh salad with a number of variations is a very good accompaniment to a cooked meal or can be eaten on its own. Remember that, to retain the vitamin content of vegetables, you should cook them for as short a time as possible. Instant mashed potatoes may be a useful standby for unexpected visits from your grandchildren.

Jacket sweetcorn bake

One 6 oz potato
2 tablespoons butter
1 tablespoon sweetcorn relish
1 tablespoon spring onion
seasoning
1 oz cheese, grated

Scrub the potato and prick its skin. Bake at 375°F for 1 hour or until soft when lightly pressed. Make a deep cross in the top. Scoop out the inside, mix with the butter, relish, onion, and seasoning. Return the mixture to its skin, top with grated cheese, and grill until golden brown.

Salad nicoise

Serves 3
lettuce, shredded
1 cup cooked whole French beans, cold
6½ oz can tunafish, drained and flaked
¼ cucumber, sliced
2 tomatoes, sliced
3 tablespoons mayonnaise or French dressing
1 hardboiled egg

Arrange the lettuce and French beans on a serving dish. Spoon the tuna into the center of the dish and surround with the cucumber and tomato slices. Pour a little French dressing over the salad and garnish with slices of hardboiled egg for a light lunch.

Lemon butter mushrooms

Serves 4
1½ cups button mushrooms
3 tablespoons butter
3 tablespoons lemon juice
½ teaspoon grated lemon rind
seasoning
1 tablespoon chopped fresh parsley

Wipe the mushrooms with a damp kitchen paper towel and place in a saucepan with the butter, lemon juice, rind, and seasoning. Cover the pan, bring to a boil, and simmer for 5 minutes. Sprinkle with parsley.

Red 'n white stir fry

Serves 4
2 tablespoons butter
1 cup red cabbage, shredded
1 cup white cabbage, shredded
2 slices bacon, grilled until crisp and finely chopped
½ teaspoon caraway seeds (optional)

Melt the butter in a large saucepan. Add the cabbage. Cook over a fairly high heat, taking care not to burn the butter, stirring constantly until the cabbage is just softened. Stir in the bacon and caraway seeds. Serve immediately.

Potato pets

mashed potatoes
For mice:
tomato puree
a few peas
a little All-Bran
some almonds
For chicks:
yellow food coloring
a few carrots and peas

Mice: Color the potato pink by adding a little tomato puree. Shape into rounds with a scoop or hands. Make a pointed nose. Use peas for the eyes and nose, almonds for the ears and All-Bran for the whiskers and the tail.
Chicks: Color the potato with yellow food coloring. Shape into rounds. Use triangles of carrot for the beak and the feet, and peas for the eyes.
Young children will be delighted by this decorative and amusing vegetable accompaniment to a main supper dish.

Jaws

Serves 4
4 potatoes, baked in their jackets
1 cup frozen peas
pat of butter
salt and pepper
8 stuffed olives, sliced

Scrub the potatoes, prick the skins, and bake at 400°F for about 1 hour. Cook the peas. Add a pat of butter. Make zigzag cuts in the side of each potato. Squeeze to open the 'mouth'. Season. Fill the potatoes with peas. Use slices of stuffed olives to make the 'eyes'. Serve with meat or fish. This vegetable dish should provide much visual entertainment.

Apple flipovers

Makes 12–14
2 eggs, separated
½ cup flour
½ level teaspoon salt
2 level teaspoons baking powder
1 level tablespoon sugar
½ cup milk
1 tablespoon melted butter *or*
   1 tablespoon vegetable oil
2 medium-size cooking apples

Sift the flour, salt, baking powder, and sugar into a bowl. Beat the egg yolks lightly and add milk and butter or oil. Add this liquid to the dry ingredients, stirring until the batter is mixed. There is no need to beat. Peel the apples and grate on a coarse grater, discarding the core. Fold in the grated apple with a large metal spoon. Beat the egg whites until stiff and fold in. Heat the griddle or pan and grease lightly. It is hot enough when a drop of water spits and splutters. Drop the batter on the hot griddle in tablespoons, allowing room for spreading. In a minute or so, when puffed and bubbly, flip over and brown the other side. Serve immediately. These flipovers are delicious for lunch or supper with sausages, bacon, or hamburgers and make a refreshing change as a 'vegetable'. You can also serve them on their own as a snack, or as a dessert.

Bon appetit!

Snacks

If your grandchildren stop by after school or come to visit for the afternoon, you may want to prepare something special for them. Here are some suggestions for scrumptious snacks. Sweet cakes should not be eaten every day, however.

Sugar can be highly addictive, and excessive intake is known to be a prime cause of dental decay and overweight, as well as causing a number of other health problems. That is why most nutritionists would recommend you do everything you can to prevent a child from developing a sweet tooth. But to deny a child sweetmeats altogether may make him crave them all the more. So try to reserve them for special occasions only, and then only one or two should be enjoyed. Never allow sweets or chocolates to replace a balanced meal. Home-made confectionery is always particularly delicious. It is not expensive to prepare, and children usually enjoy lending a helping hand.

Gingerbread men

Makes approximately 4, depending on size of cutter
4 tablespoons butter or margarine
4 tablespoons sugar
1 level tablespoon molasses
½ cup self-rising flour
1 level teaspoon ground ginger
¼ level teaspoon mixed spices
milk

Cream the butter and sugar together until light and fluffy. Beat in the molasses. Sift flour, ginger, and mixed spices onto the mixture. Fold in with a metal spoon and add a little milk if necessary. Turn onto a floured board and knead well. Roll out thinly and cut out with a shape cutter, or draw around a cardboard cutout. Carefully place on a greased baking tray. Bake in the center of the oven at 350°F for 10-15 minutes. Leave for 3-4 minutes, then transfer to a cooling tray. Decorate with sweets and piped icing.

Orange cream pots

Makes 4
2 eggs
1 tablespoon sugar
1 cup milk
grated rind of an orange
1 oz grated chocolate

Preheat the oven to 325°F. Grease four individual ovenproof dishes with butter. Whip eggs and sugar together in a bowl. Heat the milk and orange rind in a saucepan gently until amost boiling. Add to the eggs, beating constantly. Strain into another bowl and pour into the prepared dishes. Stand the dishes in a cake pan or tray and pour water two-thirds up the sides of the dishes. Bake for 20-30 minutes or until just set. Allow to cool, then chill. Decorate with grated chocolate just before serving.

Caribbean medley

Serves 4
4 slices fresh pineapple, with outside skin and core removed
2 bananas, peeled and sliced
¼ cup butter
1 oz sugar
1 tablespoon lemon juice
2 teaspoons sesame seeds

Cut the pineapple slices in half. Melt the butter in a large frying pan. When foaming, add the banana and pineapple and cook until golden. Remove from the pan and keep warm. Add the sugar, lemon juice, and sesame seeds and simmer until to the consistency of syrup. Pour over the fruit and serve immediately with ice cream or yogurt.

Egg time

Serves 3 - 6
6 hardboiled eggs
lettuce
cucumber slice
carrot sticks
red pepper
numbers cut out of paper (3,6,9,12)

Halve the eggs and arrange them on the lettuce on a large plate in the shape of a clock face. Place the cucumber slice in the center. Arrange the carrot stick clock hands. Place the numbers in appropriate positions.

Pirates' pie

Serves 6
½ cup flour
2 oz margarine
1 egg yolk

Filling
5 tablespoons lime juice cordial
½ cup seedless raisins
1 egg yolk
3 tablespoons ground almonds
2 egg whites
2 heaped tablespoons sugar
7-inch flan ring on a baking tray

Rub the margarine into the flour until the mixture resembles breadcrumbs. Bind together with the egg yolk and a little cold water, then lightly knead the pastry. Roll out on a floured surface and line the flan ring. Chill for about 15 minutes. Bake uncovered with weights to keep the crust from crumbling in a moderately hot oven at 375°F for 15 minutes. Remove weights, and bake for 5 minutes more until cooked through and a good color. Warm the lime juice and soak the raisins in it until they are plump. Stir in egg yolk and ground almonds. Fill the flan crust. Whip the egg whites stiffly, fold in the sugar, and beat again until just as stiff. Pile on top of the filling, and bake in a cool oven at 275°F for about 30 minutes until the meringue is crisp and golden brown. Serve hot or cold.

Chocolate mousse

Serves 4
6 oz dark chocolate
2 tablespoons water
4 eggs, separated
few drops of vanilla extract
whipped cream and chopped walnuts

Melt the chocolate, with water, in a large bowl over a pan of simmering water. Remove the chocolate from the heat and stir in the egg yolks and vanilla extract. Whip the egg whites until stiff and fold into the chocolate mixture. Pour into individual dishes and chill until set. Decorate the chocolate mousse with whipped cream and chopped walnuts.

Bon appetit!

For special treats, try lemon roundabouts and candy stripes, as well as the other exciting recipes suggested here.

Delicious desserts

Children always look forward to a dessert after lunch or dinner; but in no way should very sweet desserts be served every day. Nor should they be permitted if the child has not eaten a well-balanced main course. The healthiest type of dessert is a serving of fresh fruit. But the appetizing recipes that follow provide some exciting ideas for that very special treat. Ice cream is, of course, a very useful standby for desserts in case of unexpected visits from your grandchildren.

Lemon roundabouts

Makes 10 tartlets
2 tablespoons sugar
⅝ cup flour
2 tablespoons butter
2 tablespoons lard
⅝ cup cottage cheese
⅜ cup cream cheese
Lemon rind, grated
Lemon curd, for spreading (instructions follow)
1 egg, beaten

Preheat the oven to 400°F. Mix the flour, butter, and lard together in a large bowl. Add a little cold water. Knead to a dough. On a floured surface, roll out to ¼ inch thick. Using a pastry cutter, cut out ten circles. Line ten cups of a muffin tin with the circles. Mash the cottage cheese in a small bowl. Add the cream cheese, egg, sugar, and lemon rind. Fill the tartlets. Bake for 25 minutes, until golden. When cool, spread a little lemon curd over each. Lemon curd can be made from 16 tablespoons sugar, 8 tablespoons butter, the grated rind of 2 lemons, and 3 eggs. Stir all the ingredients except the eggs in a large saucepan until melted. Then add the beaten eggs and stir until the mixture thickens. Do not let it boil. You will have sufficient lemon curd to store in pots for future use.

Candy stripes

Serves 10
1 packet pineapple flavored gelatin, cubed
1 packet raspberry flavored gelatin, cubed
14 oz can of evaporated milk
1 small can pineapple chunks, drained
1 small carton raspberries, drained

Set the refrigerator on coldest setting. Put each lot of gelatin in a separate bowl and pour 1¼ cups boiling water on each. Stir until dissolved. Let cool. Pour half the evaporated milk into each bowl. Whip until thick. Spoon a little raspberry mixture into five of the glasses, and a little pineapple mixture into the other five glasses. Place the glasses in the refrigerator for 15 minutes. Spoon a second layer on top, alternating colors. Replace in the refrigerator. When set, make a third layer. Decorate with the fruit.

Butterscotch sauce

Serves 4
3 tablespoons butter
brown sugar
1 tablespoon syrup
1 teaspoon lemon juice

Heat together the butter, sugar, and syrup until the butter is melted. Boil for 1 minute and stir in the lemon juice. Serve warm, spooned over ice cream.

Bon appetit!

Traditional trifle

Serves 4
2 cups thick cream
1 orange
1 banana
1 chocolate cake, shaped like a long roll
2 pitted cherries
Optional:
2 tablespoons custard powder and 2 cups milk as an alternative to the cream

Peel a long, thin piece of rind from the orange. Cut the orange in half, and cut one slice from each half for decoration. Squeeze the juice from the orange halves. Cut the cake into round slices. If you are using custard powder, mix it with a little milk. Blend to a paste with a wooden spoon. Heat the remainder of the milk and pour it onto the blended custard. Stir. Return the mixture to the pan. Heat until thickened for two minutes. Slice the banana and place over the cake. Pour the cream or the custard over the fruit. Decorate with orange slices, orange rind, and cherries.

Swiss alpine fondue

Mandarins, small can
1 banana
1 apple
orange yogurt
4 oz plain chocolate
½ bag marshmallows
lemon juice

To make this dip, break the chocolate into pieces and place in a bowl over a pan of water on a low heat. When the chocolate has melted, gradually stir in the yogurt until the fondue is smooth. Remove from the heat, but keep the bowl over the pan. Cut the apple into quarters and remove the core. Slice thickly. Chop the banana into chunks. Sprinkle the apple and banana with a little lemon juice. Drain the mandarin oranges. Pour the fondue into a warmed dish and place on a plate. Arrange the fruit and the marshmallows around the dish and use for dipping into the fondue. It makes an excellent party dish.

Zebra crossing cake

½ cup potatoes, cooked and mashed
½ cup margarine
¾ cup sugar
few drops of vanilla extract
1 oz cocoa
3 medium eggs
¾ cup self-rising flour
2 tablespoons milk
Icing
1 cup sifted confectioners' sugar
2-3 tablespoons warm water

Place all the cake ingredients, except the cocoa, in a mixing bowl. Beat well, preferably with a mixer, until light and fluffy. Put half the mixture into a piping bag fitted with a large nozzle. Blend the cocoa with a little warm water and beat into the remaining mixture. If possible, put into a second piping bag. Pipe alternate lines of plain and chocolate mixture across the short sides of a greased 9 x 13 cake pan. If only one piping bag is available, pipe the plain mixture first, then the chocolate mixture. Gently shake pan to level the mixture. Bake at 350°F until the cake is golden brown. Cool on a wire rack. Add water to the confectioners' sugar to make glacé icing. Frost the plain bars of the cake. Decorate with cocktail stirrers made to look like beacons. These may be replaced with cocktail sticks and colored cherries to form 'traffic lights'. Place plastic figures on the crossing and toy cars next to it. Your delicious and very attractive cake now resembles a typically British pedestrian crossing, known as a 'zebra crossing' because of its characteristic white stripes.

Buttered apples

Serves 4
1½ lb cooking apples, peeled and quartered
½ cup golden raisins, and chopped dates, mixed
2 lemon slices
¼ cup brown sugar
¼ cup butter

Place the apples, dried fruit, and lemon in an ovenproof dish. Sprinkle with sugar and dot with butter. Cover and bake at 350°F for about 1 hour until the apples are soft. Serve warm with cream or plain yogurt.

Your grandchild will find this replica of a British zebra crossing both fascinating to look at and delicious to eat.

Games galore

Play of all kinds, psychologists agree, is very important for a child's all-round healthy development. In bouncing and catching a ball, he learns to master hand and eye coordination. At school, he will learn through sports to be part of a team, and through the games he plays at home, he will develop a sense of fun, as well as experiencing what it feels like both to lose and to win. Playing games with your grandchildren can provide some wonderful opportunities for imaginative activities. But don't forget the more traditional games. Some of these have been passed down through many generations and still remain childhood favorites.

Games for traveling

A long journey can be tedious for a small child unless you have at your fingertips a number of ideas for games that can be played without too much disturbance. Some will be more suitable for a car or bus trip, but others will lend themselves admirably to trips by plane, train, or ship.

What does it stand for?
Everyone in the car can play, and the winner of each round, during which each passenger has a turn, will be the one whose slogan is the most amusing or original. Simply think up a phrase or saying in which the words start with the letters on a particular car license plate that you spot. For example, WLC might stand for 'We love chocolate'. Variations on the game can be played by trying to link the names of famous people with the letters on license plates: for example, RR might stand for Roy Rogers, Robert Redford, or Ronald Reagan. There will usually be many possibilities.

The alphabet game
Going through the alphabet from A–Z, each player has to spot an object beginning with the letter of the alphabet when it is his turn: for example, A might be for 'ambulance' if one is seen, B for 'building', C for 'car', D for 'dog', and so on.

Crazy spelling
Each player, in turn, gives the next player a word to spell backwards, without using pen and paper. Start with three-letter words only, and then progress by one letter for each round. Give one point for each correct crazy spelling. This is much more difficult than you may at first think.

Towns and countries
Starting with a town beginning with the letter A, each player has to name a town beginning with the last letter of the previous word. A typical progression might be Auckland, Denver, Rome, and so on. This game can also be played using the names of countries.

How many fingers?
This is a game for two children. One player holds a hand behind his back with one or more fingers extended (include the thumb). The other player writes down in secret how many fingers he thinks the other has extended. One point is scored for each correct guess. The winner is the first to score ten points.

How far?
The idea here is for all the players to guess how far they travel in five minutes exactly. One passenger should check the time, having first noted the number on the odometer. The winner is the player who has estimated most correctly the distance actually traveled in the time.

License plate words
Each player has to spot a license-plate that spells a word with letters that can be made to spell another word. Examples might be PEA, from which you can form the word APE, or BUT from which you can form TUB.

How many words?
Pick the name of a town – Washington, for instance – and see how many words of two letters or more you can find in it (on, to, wash, go, wait, gain, and so on.)

Lipreading
This is an excellent way of keeping children quiet for a short while. Each player mouths a few words from a well-known song or saying, and the first to guess it correctly scores one point.

Can you remember?
One player starts with a phrase and the next has to repeat it, adding a phrase of his or her own. In a game for three players, the initial phrase might be "Can you remember the old lady?". The second player's line might be "Can you remember the old lady with the wooden leg?" and the third player's line "Can you remember the old lady with the

wooden leg and the long nose?" The first player's next line might be "Can you remember the old lady with the wooden leg and the long nose, who lives in Amsterdam?" and so on.

Party games

If you are called upon to assist at a small child's birthday party, as grandparents often are, you should find that the following traditional party games still delight eight-year-olds and under. They are, in fact, firm party favorites.

Pin the tail on the donkey
Draw a large picture of a donkey, without a tail. Pin it to the wall or fasten it to an easel. Make a paper tail, and put some double-sided tape or a circlet of cellophane tape on the back of it. Blindfold each player in turn. Lead each child to the donkey and get him to try to fasten the tail in its correct position.

Chinese whispers
All players should be seated in a circle. The first player whispers a short sentence into the ear of the second, and the message is passed along in soft whispers until it reaches the last player who must shout out the message. This can often be a hilarious variation on the original sentence because it has been repeatedly misheard en route.

Charades
Divide yourselves into two equal teams. One team leaves the room and thinks of the title of a book, film, play, television show, or song. They return to act out the title in total silence. Allow three minutes for each team to decide on its title, and three minutes to act it out. Score one point for a correct guess.

When grandmother went to market
This is another memory game. The first player starts: "My grandmother went to market and bought some butter". The second player continues: "My grandmother went to market and bought some butter and a green hat", and so on. The winner will be the player with the last correct complete list.

What was on the tray?
Place on a tray a variety of objects such as a teaspoon, a magazine, a key, an orange, a nut cracker, a whistle, a postage stamp, a spool of thread, a toothbrush, a bracelet, a mug, a carrot, a pencil, a flower, a candle and a bar of soap. Let everyone look at the tray for two minutes, then take it away. Each player is given paper and pencil and must try to write down all the objects that were on the tray.

Statues
You will need a piano, a radio, a cassette, or recordplayer. Play some lively music and get everyone dancing around. Suddenly turn the music off. When you do, the children have to freeze on the spot. Anyone who moves is 'out'.

Grandmother's footsteps
One player is chosen to be the 'grandmother'. He or she stands at one end of the room facing away from the others. They creep towards her. As soon as she turns around, everyone has to freeze on the spot. Anyone who moves is sent back to the other end of the room to start again. The winner is the player who touches the 'grandmother' first. He or she then takes the part of the 'grandmother'.

Squeak piggy, squeak!
The children sit cross-legged on the floor. Each is chosen in turn to come to the center and be blindfolded. The child spins round two or three times so that any sense of direction is lost. He feels his way to a child, sits on his lap, says "Squeak piggy, squeak", and has to guess on whose lap he is sitting by recognizing the squeak.

Smell it! Taste it!
Each player is blindfolded and given various foods and substances to smell in the attempt to guess what they are. You could use scented soap, lemon juice, a rose, garlic, onion, or freshly-baked bread, among many other things. As an alternative, introduce bits of food to taste, rather than to smell: for example, jam, a piece of pear, onion, honey, egg, lettuce, or cucumber. Have some tissues handy and let the children spit out the foods if they want to. Always make certain that this game is supervised so that no potentially poisonous substances are presented.

Pass the package
For this game to be played successfully, you need four or more players. Prepare the package in advance by wrapping a small present in several layers of paper. Everyone sits in a circle on the floor, passing the package around while music is playing. When you stop the music, the child holding the package at that point unwraps one layer of paper and passes it on. The child who takes off the final layer of paper receives the small present. (It may be a good idea to have some consolation prizes on hand).

Which product?
Cut out a number of familiar advertisements from newspapers and magazines, and remove the product names. Each player then has to guess the products advertised. The player with the most correct answers is the winner.

Games galore

Musical bumps
You will need a piano, a radio, cassette, or recordplayer. The children all dance around the room to the music. As soon as you stop the music, they must sit on the floor. Players who sit down before the music stops, as well as the last player to do so, are 'out'. The last player left is the winner.

Treasure hunt
You need to spend some time preparing for this game by leaving clues that lead one to another, until the 'treasure' is found. Set the rules in advance. No clues should be removed, and no player should reveal them to another. Your clues may take many forms: for instance, anagrams or riddles.

Consequences
Each player has paper and pencil. First, write down the name of a male character, followed by the word 'met'. Fold this over, and pass it to the next player, who then writes the name of a female character, followed by the word 'at'. Again, the paper is folded and passed on, with the next rounds requiring the name of a place, what he said to her, what she replied, and the consequence. The complete 'stories' are then read aloud, usually to the accompaniment of hysterical laughter.

What's in the box?
Take a large box and cut six equidistant openings around the sides, each of which should be large enough for a child's hand. Then make six divisions inside, using cardboard and tape. Seal the top of the box, and place a different object in each opening: a piece of bread, a marble, a cherry, a piece of macaroni, a lettuce leaf, and a screw, for example. Each player has to reach inside the box and guess what all the objects are, without removing them.

Indoor games

Here are some ideas for games with which to entertain your grandchildren on a rainy afternoon. There are numerous fascinating commercial games on the market, but some very entertaining times can also be had with games that require no equipment at all, simply the involvement of the players. Some may bring back memories from your own childhood.

What next?
This is a game of word associations. The first player thinks of a noun, and the next must think of something closely associated with it. For example, a simple progression might be "beach", "sea", "ship", "deck", "sailor", "water", "bucket", and so on.

Crazy cables
Think up a string of letters that are to be the initials of a telegram message. Each player must then write down a message beginning with these letters. You should find this can provide enormous fun; the more ridiculous the 'cables' are, the better.

Judge and jury
The judge faces the jury, which should consist of two or more players. One of the jury is then asked a question that he must not answer with the words "yes" or "no". He is allowed only ten seconds to reply. A player who makes the mistake of using the word "yes" or "no" or takes longer than ten seconds to answer becomes the judge in the next round that is played.

Adverbs
One of the players must leave the room. The others decide on an adverb. The first player returns and has to guess which word has been chosen by asking various questions that the others must answer in the manner of the adverb chosen. If, for example, the word 'quietly' was chosen, they would whisper all their responses.

Earth, air, and water
For this game, you need a small rubber ball. Everyone sits in a circle, with one player in the center. He throws the ball to someone and calls out either "earth", "air", or "water" as he does so. If he cries "air", the player catching the ball must immediately name something connected with the "air" – a species of bird, perhaps. If he cries "water" the player catching the ball might name a type of fish. If he cries "earth", a creature living in or on the ground might be named.

I love my love with an A
This is basically an adjective game. Each player takes a turn supplying an adjective, starting with A and working through the alphabet. The first player might provide the sentence, "I love my love with an A because she is *appealing*". The second player might say, "I love my love with a B because she is *beautiful*" and so on.

Bobbing for apples
This is a traditional Halloween game. Place a few apples in a large bowl of water. Put lots of newspaper on the floor, and put the bowl on top. Get your grandchildren to try to get the apples out of the water, using only their mouths! Or tie a length of string from one side of the room to the other. Tie a few apples to the string and get the children to bite a piece out of an apple, again without using their hands. They are bound to find this difficult, and amusing.

Games galore

Fizz, buzz
Players take turns counting from one upwards. When the number seven is reached, or any multiple of seven, or any number featuring a seven, the player whose turn it is must say "buzz" instead of the number. You can make the game more complicated by substituting the work "fizz" for five, or any multiple of five.

Throw in the cards
Find an old hat. You will also need a pack of cards. Place the hat on the floor, upside down. Each player must stand a few steps from it and will have an equal number of cards that he must try to throw into the hat. It is really not that easy!

Dotty pictures
Make ten dots on a large piece of paper. This is then passed to another player who must join them up, without crossing over any lines, in order to make a recognizable picture. To make the game more interesting for older children, increase the number of dots on the paper.

Hunt the thimble
This may be a favorite from your own childhood, and it still remains popular. Send the children out of the room or get them to promise to keep their eyes closed, and place a thimble in a position where it can be seen without moving any furniture or other objects. Call out "Hunt the thimble!" when you are ready for them to begin the search.

Simon says
Stand with the children around you, and give simple instructions like, "Simon says, raise your right hand" or "Simon says, touch your left ear". The children should follow these instructions exactly, but *not* when you intentionally fail to say "Simon says". Those who do are 'out'!

Animal, vegetable, mineral
One player thinks of an object and lets everyone else know whether it is animal, vegetable, or mineral. The players can then ask questions in order to identify the object, but these questions can be answered only by "yes" or "no". Twenty questions are allowed. The player who guesses the object correctly will select the next word. If the word is not guessed with twenty questions, the player scores a point and thinks of another object.

Concentration
This is a memory game, requiring great concentration. Spread out an entire pack of cards haphazardly and face downwards, so that no two cards overlap. Each player has to turn over two cards. If the numbers or pictures match, he takes them. If the cards do not match, they are turned face downwards again and left in their places. It is now the next player's turn. As the idea is to remember the positions of the cards so that pairs can be matched, it is important to replace the cards in the same spot. The winner is the player with the most matching pairs when all the cards have been collected.

When shopping for toys, do seek advice about the sort of games most suitable for your grandchild's age group.

Cheat!
Deal the pack of fifty-two cards to four players. The first player puts one card face downwards in the center and tells everyone what it is. The next player seated to his left places a card on top of it, again face downwards, and declares it to be one card higher (whether it is or not). If any player doubts that it really is this card, he can challenge by shouting "Cheat!" The challenged player then has to turn over his card. If it *is* the card that he said it was, the player who challenged has to take the entire pile in the center. If it is not the card, the challenged player takes all the cards in the center. The winner is the first person to put down all his cards.

Games galore

Outdoor games

When out in the yard or in a park, you might organize a few games to keep your grandchild actively amused. These may require very little by way of equipment, just a little inventiveness.

Jump over the river!
Mark off an area with two long pieces of string, widening it gradually so that towards one end the two pieces are considerably farther apart. Each player has to take a turn 'jumping the river', starting at the narrowest end and working towards the other ends of the pieces of string. The winner is the player able to jump the widest river.

Egg and spoon race
Use hardboiled eggs for this! Having chosen starting and finishing lines, give each player an egg and a spoon. The winner is the player to reach the finishing line first, with the egg balanced on the spoon, which should be held with one hand only. If a player drops his egg, he can pick it up and put it on the spoon again, but must use one hand only to do so. For a variation on the theme, get each child to run while balancing a small ball on his hand, palm-down.

Obstacle races
These can be enormous fun to organize but be careful not to make them potentially dangerous or too difficult for very small children. Let each child run the course one by one, and time him. The winner will be the player who gets around most quickly. Obstacles you could put at the various 'stops' might include a box to step into, a pair of gloves to be put on correctly, a ball to be picked up and carried, a small object to jump over, a dress to put on and take off, a stool to clamber over, and a low rope to climb under.

Wheelbarrows
This is a game that can be played by two or more children, and turned into a race if there are four or any larger even number. One of each pair must get down on the ground, his partner picking up his legs. The player on the ground then 'walks' along as quickly as possible, using only his hands. His feet must not touch the ground.

Jump the bean bag
Tie a bean bag to a piece of rope. This is easily made by sewing up three sides of a 6-inch square of fabric and inserting three handfuls of dried beans before sewing up the fourth side. Get the children to stand in a circle, and swing the rope round. Everyone should jump over the rope, without touching the bean bag. Take care not to turn too quickly or you may get dizzy!

Easter egg hunt
Early on Easter Sunday morning, hide small decoratively wrapped chocolate eggs in the garden, and let the children hunt for them. They can keep those that bear their initials. Make sure that there are some for everybody!

I spy
This a quiet game for the car or yard and an exercise in observation. One player starts by saying "I spy, with my little eye, something beginning with", and the others have to guess what it is he can see.

Crazy golf
Make your own crazy golf course by constructing a series of obstacles using cardboard boxes, old cans, large cardboard tubes, and other objects through or around which the ball has to be hit. You can build an alley, slopes, arches, and a variety of other challenging hazards in this way.

Sevens
This is a game that can be played by a child on his or her own. All that is needed is a small ball and a wall. The aim is to throw the ball against the wall and to catch it in seven different ways. Here are some examples: throwing the ball against the wall and letting it bounce before it is caught; throwing the ball against the wall and catching it without it bouncing; spinning round before catching it; and catching the ball with the left hand only.

It's magic!

Children adore magic, and are usually happy to spend hours either mastering their own tricks or watching you provide some examples of wizardry. Here are a few beginners' ideas for some hocus-pocus. Show the young magician how to present his act with confidence, and give him examples of the effective use of patter while he does his tricks. There are some excellent books of magic tricks available, as well as conjuring sets, which you can use to extend the repertoire.

Guessing the coin
You need a handkerchief, four coins of different value, a mug, and an accomplice! Beforehand, agree with the accomplice that if he places the mug with its handle in a certain direction, that particular direction will indicate that a coin of a particular value is under the cup. Invite the audience to place one of the coins on the handkerchief while you are out of the room, and get your accomplice to place the mug over it. Then you can return and reveal the value of the coin correctly, simply by looking at the position of the mug's handle.

The name trick
Ask each person in the audience to think of someone's name and to shout it out. You explain that you will write down all the names on pieces of paper and put them into a hat. Then, through concentration, you will reveal which name is picked out of the hat by someone in the audience. However, what you actually do is write down the first name that was called out on every piece of paper, so that the name picked out of the hat could only be that one.

The non-bursting balloon
Prepare the balloon in advance by putting two pieces of clear tape across one another on each side of the balloon. Then stick a knitting needle through the balloon, taking care to do so at the points where the tape is stuck, saying some magic words. The audience should be amazed that the balloon does not burst, and will not see the tape as it is clear.

The disappearing glass
You will need an accomplice for this. Place a glass under a handkerchief, and invite everyone to feel that it is in position. When the last person has felt the glass, you can throw the handkerchief in the air and show that the glass has disappeared. The last person to touch the glass must be the accomplice. As he comes up to touch the glass, he should secretly remove and hide it.

The magic ticket
The idea of this trick is to tear up a ticket into several pieces, say the magic words, and then find that the bits have joined together again so that the 'original' ticket is perfect. The ticket that you prepare beforehand actually consists of two identical tickets. One is folded up very small and pasted on the back of the other. This can then be opened out and presented as the restored ticket.

Secret codes

Teach your grandchild not only how to send secret messages in code but also how to crack codes, and you should have a great deal of fun together.

Skip two letters
One simple way to conceal a message is to insert two random letters between the real letters that make up the words of the message. Thus Z A M L B E G R E I U T N O M B Q E X L B R U Y T O T L U H F R E R F T W I R O T E L L E reads "Meet me by the tree". You can vary this theme by alternating the number of letters to be skipped, perhaps one and then two, then one again, and so on; or first one, then two, then three, and then four, and so on.

Number codes
You can also send secret messages by devising a simple number code, whereby each number stands for a letter. The numbers chosen need not necessarily relate to the position of the letters in the alphabet. That would be too simple. Instead, choose a sentence that contains most, if not all of the letters in the alphabet. "The quick brown fox jumps over the lazy dog" is a good example. T would be represented by the number 1, H by 2, E by 3, and so on. Using this sentence, the code message 9,10,5,13,26,17,3,10,1,2,3,17,10,13,3,24 would be transcribed as "Bring me the money".

Book codes
You will first need to decide on a particular book to use as the basis for solving each coded message. If the messages are being sent by mail, you and your 'secret agent' will both need a copy of the same book. Each word of the message will be represented by a series of three numbers: the first number stands for the page in the book, the second for the line (counting from the top), and the third for a particular word in the line (counting from the left).

Wild flowers
You can send messages, too, by stringing together a series of words, the only words relevant to the message being those that come after the name of a flower. Thus, GREEN HOUSE ROSE LEAVE DANGER RED CARNATION LONDON PAPER NEXT WEEK BLUEBELL IMMEDIATELY BLUE reads "Leave London immediately".

A picture code
Here is another code idea for secret agents who like drawing. Together with your grandchild, write down all the letters of the alphabet, and by the side of each sketch an object that begins with that letter: an arrow for A, a boat for B, a cat for C, and so on. Messages can then be sent in picture form.

Morse code
Invented by Samuel Morse in the nineteenth century, this sort of code consists of an alphabet of dots and dashes. Using a torch, a short flash can equal a dot, and a longer flash corresponds to a dash.

A .-	I ..	Q --.-	Y -.--	7 --...
B -...	J .---	R .-.	Z --..	8 ---..
C -.-.	K -.-	S ...	1 .----	9 ----.
D -..	L .-..	T -	2 ..---	0 -----
E .	M --	U ..-	3 ...--	full stop .-.-.-
F ..-.	N -.	V ...-	4 ....-	comma --..--
G --.	O ---	W .--	5	question mark ..--..
H	P .--.	X -..-	6 -....	

Choosing Toys

If you are new to the role of grandparent, it may be years since you last went into a toy store. Be prepared for something of a surprise. There are now so many different toys that finding a suitable Christmas or birthday gift can easily become a confusing experience. The difficulty lies in assessing correctly what is right for a child at his or her particular stage of development or for his or her special interests. Safety, too, is an all-important factor. Read on for advice about choosing toys that are really worthwhile buys.

There are many fads and fashions as far as toys are concerned. Only recently, for instance, there have been reports of parents fighting over limited supplies of Cabbage Patch dolls, which come complete with adoption certificates. Children may try to persuade you to buy them a toy that is the very latest craze; that is only natural. But the best toys are undoubtedly those that encourage the development of both imagination and coordination. They should also be well made. Test the toy *before* you buy it, and ask yourself these questions. Is it safe? Does it work? Will it break easily? Will your grandchild soon tire of it? Can your grandchild do more than one thing with it, or does it have only limited possibilities for play of a truly creative nature?

The first six months

For the first few weeks of a baby's life, toys mean very little. Your infant grandchild's focusing distance will be limited for a while, and once it develops he will want to concentrate at first on the faces of those around him rather than on playthings. After about three months, however, he will begin to enjoy toys designed to be watched, and also those that can be listened to: mobiles, stuffed animals, rattles, music boxes, colorful pictures, and soft, bright-colored blocks. He will be able to hold things, too, if only for a few seconds. Any rattle you buy should be lightweight, washable, unbreakable, and, if possible, have a handle to facilitate grasping. Soon, too, he will be enthralled by a special baby mirror for his crib. A 'busy box' with knobs to turn or push should provide many happy hours of play and increase his manipulative skills. Anything that your grandchild can safely bite on will also be welcomed, not just because he may be teething but because putting things into the mouth is one of a baby's natural ways of exploring his world.

Towards the first birthday

By the second half of his first year, your grandchild will enjoy playing with cups that stack, as well as toys that squeak, bang, or make some other noise – a music box or a drum, perhaps. Whenever you give noisy toys to a child of any age, you and his parents will of course have to be patient listeners. It is unfair to the child to keep taking the toy away in order to enjoy some peace and quiet. Towards his first birthday, too, you will find that he particularly enjoys throwing toys on to the floor for someone to pick up. *You* will tire of this soon enough but your grandchild could probably keep at it for hours! Tying toys to his high chair or stroller could save you a bad back or aching knees. Now that he is more mobile, he will also enjoy toys that can be pushed and pulled. He may even be able to start using crayons if his dexterity is sufficiently advanced.

Small babies enjoy watching mobiles. Later, cuddly toys and construction kits are likely to become firm favorites, too.

The second year

As your grandchild's coordination improves, he will welcome many more toys. Simple musical instruments, like a xylophone or a toy piano, wooden puzzles with large pieces that interlock easily, hammer-and-peg toys, wooden blocks to build, knock down and reconstruct, animals on wheels, construction sets with large component parts, and toys that require the matching of shapes will all contribute positively to the development of his manipulative skills. Bath toys continue to be fun, as do dolls, cars, and soft toys. Bricks sold with a truck will not only provide the building blocks for imaginary towers and houses but they can also be wheeled along by your grandchild as he masters the art of walking. Paints and paper will amuse a child for long periods at this age. Protect both your table and the floor with newspaper or a waterproof covering. You and your grandchild will need paint smocks, too, to prevent your clothes from becoming paint-stained.

Imitative and creative play

After his second birthday, a child will benefit most from toys that teach him something about his environment. This is also the stage at which children like to copy adult behavior; so, not unexpectedly, games that involve adult occupations are very popular with this age group. A toy tea set, a dollhouse, a doll's cradle and buggy, puppets, and cars all make excellent props for imitative games. Three and four-year-olds will also enjoy learning to ride a tricycle or again, copying adults, by riding in a toy car. Miniature adult games with a bat and ball are also usually well received.

Not all toys have to be exact replicas of the real thing. Give a child a model train, and that is what it will always be to him. A more 'abstract' vehicle on wheels can, with a little imagination, become a bus, a rocket launching pad, a train, a car, or a truck. A simple piece of cloth can be turned into a tent or a wizard's cloak. A cardboard box can be a ship, a doll's bed, or a castle; several boxes can make a train. As you will see, it is not always the most expensive or sophisticated toys that are the most successful with small children.

Truly creative play may help your grandchild in areas where he is not as forthcoming as he might be. The shy and retiring child, for example, might benefit from playing at being rancher to a herd of cows, teacher to a class of dolls, or perhaps commander of a space station. There are many benefits that a careful choice of toys can bring.

Paint and paper

Paints, crayons, and modeling clay are always favorites with children. But the best sort of paints for a small grandchild aren't necessarily those that come in tiny palettes in a metal box. Toddlers need to paint with bright colors and to make large shapes. Poster paints are best, and so are large brushes. You should be able to find nonspill plastic jars with a hole in the top for the brush, but even an old egg carton can be turned into a young artist's palette. Sponges, cotton swabs, cork, or a piece of potato can all be used as painting tools and substitutes for a brush. Wallpaper, brown wrapping paper, and old newspapers are suitable surfaces to paint on. Your grandchild will have a wonderful time with fingerpaints, too, but keep him away from the walls before he rinses those hands!

You might ask your grandchild if you can keep some of his drawings and pin them up at home. Nothing will please him or her more than to see

Choosing toys

them displayed this way, or used as birthday or Christmas cards, or for a calendar. Coloring books can provide an occasional novelty but there is nothing more beneficial to creativity than for a child to fashion his own paintings and drawings. Crayons, felt tips, and a black board and colored chalks make excellent drawing materials, too. You may not recognize what your grandchild's works depict at first, but encourage him or her with these first creative efforts. Let him tell you what he feels about his drawings, but avoid making specific remarks yourself. Maximize his feelings of enjoyment and satisfaction so that he creates to please himself, not you.

Too many toys?

The toddler who has a playroom full of toys may become so confused by them that he never learns to explore the full potential of each. Don't give a child too many toys at once. Keep a few toys at your home for when he or she comes to visit, and rotate these, too. Bring out some one week, and some another. That way, your grandchild will not tire of them too quickly and may rediscover the delights of a particular toy all over again. Don't forget either that by overwhelming a child with toys, you are in danger of leading him to expect things. The most generous gift you could give is not necessarily the most expensive. Instead, it is the one you have chosen with infinite care and your concern that it will occupy him in an absorbing and enjoyable way. Avoid overpriced five-minute wonders; the chances are that your grandchild will be bored with them in no time and that you, in turn, will resent the hole they have burned in your pocket.

The second and subsequent children in a family will tend to have more toys as they are passed down; but that's not to say they shouldn't be bought anything new. Children need to learn to respect their possessions, and there is something special to a toddler about a toy that has been chosen specifically for him.

Choosing a gift for your grandchild will undoutedly be a great pleasure: but don't be disappointed if you do not always get the reaction you anticipated. Given presents to undo, toddlers often find greater delight in the package's wrapping than in the toy itself. Sometimes, too, they are simply not in the mood to play and will need time to become acquainted with the toy and the way in which it functions. If your small grandchild seems reluctant to play with what you have bought for him or even throws it aside, don't automatically assume that you have chosen the wrong thing. The pleasure in seeing him enjoy the new toy may simply have to be postponed for a while.

The comforter

However many toys a small child has, there is usually one item – most often a soft toy but sometimes just a piece of cloth – that becomes a firm favorite, even to the extent that the toddler will not leave the house without it. In many ways, this use of a 'comforter' seems to mark the transition between the constant need for mother and the desire to let go. When you are looking after your grandchild, remember that he may need his 'comforter' with him and that a substitute may simply not suffice.

Favorite childhood toys are hard to part with, and many of us keep at least one until well into adulthood. Parents often find it hard to part with their children's toys, too. Take a look in the attic. You might have some toys that your own family played with, or even some that *you* had as a child. It might be fun to bring them out when your grandchild visits. (It could, incidentally, be a profitable search because certain toys are now collectors' items and might bring as much as a hundred times their original purchase price at an auction or through a dealer).

Play safe

It can be terribly disappointing – even, in extreme cases, tragic – if a toy, bought and given with great love, causes an accident in some way. Whenever you choose playthings for your grandchild, be safety conscious. Here are some points to bear in mind, from the cradle onwards.

First of all, never let your small grandchild play with any toys that are so small he can swallow them. All babies put things in their mouths as a normal part of development and early play, and an infant could easily choke on something like a bead, or he might try to push it up his nose or into his ear. The size of a toy is very important as far as a baby is concerned.

Check that any toy that is painted is nontoxic. Since babies so often explore objects with their mouths, it is essential that any paint used is lead-free. This also applies to paint used for children's furniture.

Toys made from very thin plastic are not a wise purchase. They tend to break easily, and the broken parts may have dangerously sharp edges. In general, avoid toys that have any hard edges on which your grandchild might scratch himself.

Even when you are choosing a soft toy, there are still certain safety aspects to bear in mind. The presence of a special safety label, guaranteeing standards, will help you make a wise purchase but not all manufacturers provide them. Examine the bear, rabbit, or whatever soft toy you are considering to check that there are no sharp pieces of wire that are likely to protrude, and that the eyes and nose are well fastened to the fabric. Soft toys should also be washable.

When choosing crayons for a toddler, check that they are nontoxic. It will also be wise to see they are not too tempting. A six-year-old recently died after swallowing a bright-colored, fruit-flavored pen top that he had been sucking.

You need to see that your small grandchild is well supervised when playing and left in your charge. If he is using a walker, for instance, you must see that there are no electrical cords that might trip him. See, too, that any riding toy is stable, and that your grandchild is sitting far enough forwards so that it doesn't tip back. You also need to see that he is strapped into any indoor swing with a separate safety harness. Don't leave him alone in a bouncer, either.

If you ever buy your grandchild sparklers or fireworks, never let him or her play with them unsupervised. All fireworks should be lit by an adult, and the instructions followed very carefully. Firework displays can be tremendous fun, but should be enjoyed only from a safe distance.

The most simple of toys can be entertaining, but safety should always be considered first. Plastic bags in particular can be extremely dangerous, and no child should ever play with them for fear of suffocation.

For boys or girls?

Grandparents are sometimes a little puzzled by a child's choice of toy but there should be no cause for concern if you find, for instance, that your three-year-old grandson likes playing with dolls or that a four-year-old girl would like a train set. Small boys quite commonly enjoy playing with dolls. This is not a sign of effeminate behavior, but imitative play. Several toy manufacturers have cottoned on to the fact, successfully selling a range of male dolls that can be dressed in a variety of outfits. Similarly, the girl who enjoys playing with construction sets should not be discouraged from doing so. There are no strict rules for the suitability of toys for one sex or the other, just as it is really not possible to class toys accurately by age, but only to give guidelines.

Something from nothing

Not all your grandchild's toys have to come from a store. There are many things you can make for him or her, using only the most basic of equipment. On pages 42-51, you will find a number of ideas for playthings that can be put together quickly and cheaply. But ordinary household objects, too, can be a source of fascination to a baby. Toddlers enjoy playing with wooden and plastic spoons, icecube trays, egg cartons, old baking pans, the cardboard tubes inside toiletpaper and paper towel rolls, balls of wool and string, and sponges. Save old plastic containers for games in the bath; and use one, too, with rice, beans, or macaroni to make a rattle, making sure that it cannot be opened. The possibilities are endless.

Winning and losing

Board and other games that present an element of competition have a particularly valuable lesson to offer. How to win and how to accept losing are important lessons to master, and if this can be done through play, so much the better. The toddler who will not give up his bat for the next child's turn or the child who throws a tantrum in sheer rage at not winning will soon learn how unpopular this makes him with peers, parents and grandparents alike.

In a sense, practical jokes come into this category, too, since the one who plays the joke is very much the 'winner'. They can be marvelously entertaining But it is a good idea to make certain rules in advance if things are not to go too far. A rubber spider placed on an adult's plate will probably be amusing and do no harm but point out that it could easily be swallowed by a younger brother or sister. Similarly, a 'pretend' fried egg or chocolate biscuit could perhaps break a tooth if bitten, and a truly horrific mask could give someone very elderly or infirm a dangerous shock. Play some practical jokes on your grandchild, too, from time to time. It will do him no harm to know what it is like to be on the receiving end. In fact, he will probably want to try them out immediately on someone else.

The young bookworm

Most toddlers love books, and you can encourage an interest in them almost as soon as your grandchild is able to hold one. There are many stiff board or rag books with vibrantly colored, bold pictures and no words at all that have been designed with infants in mind. Provide as wide a variety as possible but don't expect the books to be kept in perfect condition before a child is old enough to understand the concept of respect for possessions. Far better that he turns the pages and looks at the illustrations, even if he does chew at the corners or mark the pages, than not to have this exciting stimulus. Once he enjoys being read to and begins to master the art himself, you could choose books together. He may even be able to have his own library card, by which time, of course, he must be aware of the importance of caring for books, and particularly those that are

Choosing toys

Toddlers love painting large shapes in bright colors.

not actually his property. Pop-up books are enjoying popular revival and are a source of delight to adults and children alike. Many books also have moving parts, but these cannot be handled roughly if they are to remain in working order. They are therefore usually more suitable for a child who already appreciates books.

From time to time, you may be surprised at the sort of books your grandchild chooses – stories that you feel might give him nightmares, or books with illustrations that you think will terrify him. If, however, your grandchild has chosen the book himself, the chances are he will not be worried by its content and if he is, he will probably say so. But if you feel anxious about the content of a particular title, it may be sensible either to consult with his parents first or to encourage him to choose another book.

Reading aloud to a small grandchild will help him to learn to follow a story line and should develop his imagination; but don't be surprised if you are asked to repeat the very same story again and again. Children often find it comforting to hear the same tale several times over, and may even correct you if you attempt to shorten it or to use different words. Once a child is particularly fond of a certain character in a series, you will usually find that he will try to get all the titles available. Check with your grandchild's parents as to whether he already has a certain book if you are buying one for a present. An attractive nursery rhyme book is often a successful present as it brings together many of the elements children appreciate – singing, dancing, repetition, and pictures.

Look for books of puzzles and games, as well as nonfiction titles that will expand your grandchild's interest in a particular subject or hobby. A set of encyclopedias may look very nice on the bookshelves but if they are to be put to good effect, make sure your grandchild knows how to use the index and encourage him to look things up. Knowing how and where to find relevant information is an important skill to be mastered in childhood, and will help tremendously at school.

Useful toys

Now that so many families have home computers, an educational software program or a computer game can make a very special present. These sophisticated 'toys' can be used to teach letter and number recognition, judging and comparison of shape, length, and height, and many other skills, and are suitable for children from three years of age onwards. But before you invest in one of these programs, check that it will be compatible with the particular make of computer with which it would be used. Most of the learning programs are designed for an adult's participation, too; so if you are one of the pre-computer generation, working and playing with your grandchild on a home computer in this way should give you the opportunity to catch up on basics!

Construction kits make excellent gifts for grandchildren of an older age group. Some are extremely complex to put together, and your assistance may be required. A bicycle is always a greatly appreciated present but, as always, do your homework first and check that it is indeed something that your grandchild's parents feel happy about.

Look out for toys with a health purpose, too. In the U.K., for example, one go-ahead company is marketing a musical toothbrush, which has a music box in the handle. Even when wound up, this ingenious 'toy' will not operate until the right amount of pressure is applied or the correct up and down movement made. It then runs for about one-and-a-half minutes, the time recommended for brushing the upper or lower set of teeth, so a repeat performance is required.

Choosing toys

Toys for outdoors

Some toys are particularly suitable for children with yards. A sandbox, for example, makes an excellent play area. They are available either in wood or plastic, and usually have seats in the corners. Or you could perhaps make one in wood. Provide a bucket, a spade, and other suitable tools, and your two or three-year-old grandchild will be in his element.

Most children from three to six years would also enjoy an outdoor playhouse of some kind. Ready-made playhouses are usually quite expensive, so you could keep an eye open for a secondhand one or make a simpler version for your grandchild, using a wooden or metal frame with a cloth covering, or even just a large cardboard box. Playhouses can provide countless hours of entertainment for young children.

Physical play is extremely important for the growing child, and most swinging, leaping, and jumping is best done outside. A jungle gym makes an excellent yard toy; but whether you buy the frame ready-made or put one together yourself, make sure that it is really stable once erected. Similarly, you need to be very careful about the safety of a swing, particularly if it is an improvised homemade model. The best sort of swing for a toddler is one with safety bars, so that he has to be lifted in and out of it. Check that its base is stable. A teeter-totter, too, provides an opportunity for balancing play, as does a trampoline. Kites and roller skates often make successful gifts. Ball and bat games for the yard or park are always popular. But remember, if you are invited to join in, that what makes a game "good" from a child's point of view is for him, at least some of the time, to be the winner!

Do check on the safety aspects of all toys that you buy.

The very best toys develop both imagination and coordination.

Pride in possessions

Try, if you can, to get your grandchild to take pride in his or her possessions. Toys should be tidied away at the end of a day's play and not left about on the floor where they could easily be tripped over and thus be a danger to everyone in the family. A toy chest is an excellent piece of storage equipment for the playroom, and can be easily made. All too often, such things as bricks and bits of jigsaw puzzles get mislaid. Try to encourage your grandchild to keep sets together, so that games are not ruined because of missing pieces. Marking the backs of jigsaw pieces so that they can be readily identified should help in this respect.

You may well find that your grandchild, as a toddler, is reluctant to share his toys with either a sibling or a friend. The art of sharing is definitely something that a child has to come to learn, and there will probably be a few upsets on the way. But if you can show your grandchild that sharing is something that can work in both directions and that his own possessions will be returned before too long, the experience should not be too painful.

Remember to take a look in the cupboards where you put things into store to see whether you still have a few toys that belonged to your own children, and perhaps even some that you used to play with as a child. Toys enjoyed by previous generations are particularly fascinating, and toy museums can provide a great deal of entertainment for adults and children alike.

Encourage your grandchild to treasure his or her toys. Even the most simple of playthings could perhaps become heirlooms that future generations will enjoy in the same way, too.

First aid

It is especially important to have a good first aid manual at home when you have young children about. A first aid course, organized by local groups of certain accident prevention organizations, or evening classes will provide good practical training and will give you the confidence to cope with all sorts of situations. Here, meanwhile, are a few tips for any emergencies and some essential contents for your medicine chest.

The medicine cabinet

This should be well out of reach of toddlers and have a childproof lock. Ensure that it contains only items that are needed; and always flush away drugs and tablets that are no longer required. Ask that all prescribed medicines be given to you in childproof bottles. Items that the cabinet might usefully contain are:

cotton tipped swabs/ (sterile) gauze squares/scissors/ safety pins/antihistamine cream (for stings)/children's aspirin substitute/an antiseptic for cleaning a wound/ calamine lotion/milk of magnesia (for stomach upsets)/ sun cream /thermometer/square-ended tweezers/freshly laundered and sterile handkerchief, kept in a sealed plastic bag/bandages.

Cuts and bruises

Children bruise frequently because of falls and other mishaps. Minor bruising will clear up on its own. There is no need to adopt the old fashioned remedy of rubbing in butter: but a cold compress or ice pack may help relieve any swelling. Severe bruising should, however, be shown to a doctor. All cuts and grazes should be thoroughly cleansed with an antiseptic. If you do not have any on hand, dissolve a teaspoon of salt in a glass of water. Dress the wound. There are decorative bandages available that toddlers love, so you may want to have some in your first aid supplies. If a cut is very deep, either see a doctor or take your grandchild to the emergency room of the nearest hospital. To stop severe bleeding, press firmly on the flesh above the wound (that is, closest to the heart). It will also help to raise the injured limb above heart level.

If you suspect that your grandchild is showing signs of having a great many accidents, encourage his parents to see the doctor. There might be an emotional cause, or a coordination problem.

Bites, blisters, and burns

It will be essential to know the date of the last tetanus injection if your grandchild has the unfortunate experience of being bitten by a dog or other animal, and the doctor must be consulted. Bites on the face and neck will be of particular concern. In case of snake bites, you should consult the doctor, hospital, or poison center immediately. Have your grandchild lie down, and see that he does not move around.

Blisters should not be pricked. Let them go away on their own, perhaps covering them lightly with gauze. No further treatment is necessary.

Even if you take all possible safety precautions, your grandchild could still suffer a burn or scald from hot liquids or as a result of approaching a stove or fire. If it is a minor burn, simply hold it under cool, running water to ease the pain and cover the area with clean gauze. Don't apply butter, soap, or creams; these will not help at all. For more severe burns, you should take your grandchild to the nearest emergency room. Keep him or her as calm as possible. If clothing catches fire, roll the child in a rug or blanket and pour on cold water. Don't attempt to remove any burned clothing unless the burn is due to scalding with a liquid. In this instance, remove the clothes and wrap the child in a clean sheet before taking him or her to hospital. As for sunburn, prevention, as always, is better than cure.

Sprains and fractures

It can often be difficult to determine when there is a break or a fracture, so seek medical advice. A sprain may occur in the arm or leg, and there will usually be pain on moving any swelling. It is essential to prevent strain on the affected area, which may need support in a comfortable position.

If you suspect a fracture – after a bad fall, for instance – it is essential not to move your grandchild any more than absolutely necessary. Deal with any external bleeding first and if medical help is delayed, make a padded splint with a walking stick or umbrella, wrapped and tied alongside but well above and below the suspected break. It should be fastened securely enough not to permit movement of the fractured limb but must permit the flow of blood. A greenstick fracture, particularly common in children, is a fracture along one side of a bone only.

Electric shock

First of all, switch off the current. If this is not possible, take care not to touch your grandchild or you may get a shock, too. Break the contact by using something that will not conduct electricity: a wooden chair, for instance. If he is unconscious, place him in the recovery position, as described in the section headed 'Bringing him round'. Any electrical burn should be seen by a doctor.

Stings and splinters

Wasp and bee stings are best removed with tweezers or a needle, after bathing the affected area with cotton swabs soaked in bicarbonate of soda. If the sting is in the mouth, consult a doctor immediately or take your grandchild to the nearest hospital. A cold drink to sip or an ice cube to suck will ease the discomfort. Any signs of an allergic response swelling, vomiting, or dizzy spells should be reported to the doctor as soon as possible, as should any multiple stings.

Splinters or slivers are best removed with a needle that has been sterilized by passing it through a flame a few times. Warn your grandchild that it may hurt a little. Hold the area of skin steady and, once the needle has cooled, break the skin gently at the end of the splinter. Use tweezers to pull it out, and then clean the area with an antiseptic or salt solution. There will be no need to apply a bandage.

Nosebleeds

Children quite often suffer from nosebleeds, usually caused either by constant picking or damage during play. If it occurs, hold your grandchild's head down, and place pressure on either side of the nose until the bleeding stops. Make sure that he does not lie flat but sits up. If bleeding occurs very frequently, seek medical advice. It is not a major cause for concern, but can be a disturbing experience for the young.

The perils of poisons

If you suspect that your grandchild has swallowed something poisonous, seek immediate medical help. Many cities have a poison control hotline number where you can get advice immediately. Keep this number by the phone. If it is pills or medicine, take the child to a hospital or to a poison center and bring along the container. If the child has swallowed a household poison – bleach, paraffin, or weed killer, for instance – give him water to drink to dilute the substance swallowed, but on no account give salt water in an attempt to make him sick. Then take him to the hospital and bring a sample of the substance he has swallowed with you.

Choking and shock

If your grandchild chokes, hold him upside down and slap his back fairly smartly between the shoulder blades or shake him up and down. (Peanuts and boiled sweets are a particular danger as far as choking is concerned.) An alternative method is to lay the baby on his back, put both hands round him as if to embrace him and give three or four hard pushes with your thumbs below the ribs. The same method can be adopted for an older child, but sit him up in a chair. If this is not successful, try putting your finger down his throat or seek medical help promptly.

A child suffering from mild shock, after a fright or injury, will be shaky, with perhaps sweaty, clammy skin and a pale face. Have him lie down calmly, with his head lower than his feet, to ensure that adequate blood is passing to the brain. Cover him with a rug or blanket, and place his head to one side so that if he reacts by vomiting, he will not choke. Don't give him anything to eat or drink until he is feeling better. More acute shock, with symptoms of giddiness, blurred vision, and rapid, shallow breathing, will need medical attention.

Injuries to eyes and ears

Any dust in the eyes will usually come out quite naturally when the eyes water: but if anything else enters the eye, it should be teated by a doctor. If it is a chemical of some kind, pour water over the eye for a few minutes and take your grandchild to the nearest emergency room, bringing the substance with you. Stop your grandchild from rubbing his eyes and do not apply a dressing. Any foreign body in the ear should also be removed by a doctor in order to avoid risk of damage to the eardrum.

Bringing him round

Always place an unconscious child in the recovery position. Turn him onto his side, and place his upper arm so that it is at right angles to his body, bending his elbow. Draw up his thigh so that it also forms a right angle, and bend his knee. Check that his mouth and nose are not blocked, that his tongue has not fallen to the back of his mouth and that clothing is loose. Artificial respiration (mouth-to-mouth) will be necessary if he is not breathing. Or try external cardiac massage. Put the heel of your hand or your fingers on his breast bone and press for about a second, repeating in a regular rhythm. Send someone to seek immediate medical help.

Grandma, I don't feel well!

However fit and healthy your grandchild may be, there are bound to be days when he doesn't feel well, and it may be up to you to take care of him at such a time. If it has been some time since you nursed a sick child, a brief refresher course should prove useful.

It is sometimes quite hard to assess just how serious children's complaints are. But, in general, you would be wise to seek immediate medical advice in any of the following instances:

- if your grandchild has a fever of over 100°F and is hot, restless, and perhaps delirious. But watch for other symptoms as a slightly elevated temperature may be due simply to overactivity. A low temperature can also be a cause for concern, particularly in an infant; 97.5°F to 99.5°F is the range of normal temperature.
- if he faints.
- if he has any form of convulsion or fit.
- if he has violent stomach pains that make him scream out or double up.
- if he has very bad earache.
- if a small baby will not eat or has difficulty in breathing.
- if he vomits or has diarrhea, with greater loss of fluid than he is taking in.

The complaint may not be serious at all, but it is better to consult a doctor in case there is need for prompt treatment. If you telephone your doctor at night, he may set your mind at rest, advise you to wait until morning, or suggest you take your grandchild to the emergency department of the nearest hospital.

It is usually best not to take a small child's temperature by mouth as he might bite the glass. Instead, if you know how to use this method, take his temperature rectally, placing the baby on this back, holding his legs up and a little apart, and inserting the thermometer about one inch into the rectum for two minutes. It will help to have first lubricated the thermometer with baby oil. Or, when taking the temperature of an older child, place the mercury end of the thermometer in his armpit and place his arms across his chest to hold the thermometer in position for two or three minutes. Your pharmacist may also stock special heat strips that can be placed on a child's forehead to register temperature, but these will not be quite as accurate as a thermometer reading. You can also get a good indication of whether your grandchild has a temperature by feeling his forehead with the back of your hand. If he does have a fever, keep the room at a moderate temperature, 67°F or so, keep him lightly clothed in bed, and sponge him down with tepid water, leaving his skin damp. If the fever persists, or if he has a febrile convulsion, call the doctor. Meanwhile, stay with your grandchild and comfort him. Do not give aspirin to lower the temperature. It has been implicated in cases of Reye's Syndrome following a viral infection where aspirin was used. If you feel the child needs something, doctors recommend using *acetaminophen* (Tylenol® is one brand).

Coughs and colds

Small children are prone to colds that often make them feel uncomfortable since they have difficulty blowing their noses. For a particularly severe infection of this kind, a doctor may recommend nose drops; but you should not continue to give them any longer than recommended and you should never give them to your grandchild unless they have been prescribed. A small child's cough may be perturbing, but a productive cough, which helps him clear out mucus, has a useful function. However, it may be wise to consult a doctor if the cough continues for more than a couple of days. For an unproductive, irritating cough, a doctor may prescribe a suppressant of some kind, suitable for children.

Aches and pains

A stomachache is a familiar childhood problem, but sometimes an imaginary one, serving as an excuse, as you will probably recall only too well. The trouble is that you should take any such complaint seriously because stomach pains can be a sign of something fairly critical. If your grandchild shrieks or curls up in agony, or if the pain does not subside after a while, call the doctor, particularly if there is also fever, diarrhea, or sickness. The pain that heralds appendicitis usually starts around the umbilicus or belly button, and then moves to the lower right. At times, stomachaches can have emotional causes. If you suspect this may be the case, try to find out what is bothering him.

Another fairly common complaint in childhood is earache. A word of warning: never probe anything into your grandchild's ear, as this may easily cause damage. Nor should you apply external heat in an attempt to provide comfort.

Grandma, I don't feel well!

This refresher course will be useful if it is some years since you last cared for a sick child.

Instead, seek a doctor's advice. The pain may be due to inflammation, in which case antibiotics or drops may be prescribed, or it may be due to changes in atmospheric pressure or to a foreign body in the ear. Toothache or an infection of the gums may also sometimes be experienced as pain in the region of the ear.

It is often quite hard to diagnose the cause of a headache in a child. Try sympathy, pure and simple, to start with, just in case it has been brought on by the prospect of some unpleasant event. But if it continues, it may be the prelude to some childhood illness, or due to toothache or swollen glands. Do be sure to consult the doctor if you are at all in doubt.

Stomach upsets

A balanced diet, with plenty of fruit and vegetables to provide fiber, should prevent constipation. But some children empty their bowels only every two or three days, so there is no need to become obsessed with regularity. You will be better able to assess whether your grandchild is constipated by judging consistency rather than frequency. Stools that are dry, hard, and painful to pass are a sure indication. In a baby, constipation may be due to lack of fluid; diluted fruit juice may help. Never give laxatives without a doctor's prescription. They could prove quite harmful to a child's system.

Diarrhea may be due to food poisoning, illness of some kind, or perhaps to an emotional upset. It can be serious in a small baby, and every care must be taken to ensure that there is sufficient intake of fluid to replace what is lost. Offer cooled, boiled water to the infant, and consult your doctor promptly. If a child is not eating, has a fever, and vomits, call your doctor, too. Very serious gastroenteritis may require hospitalization; but for milder cases, a fluid diet for a couple of days may be all that is required. The doctor will advise you what to feed while the illness persists. Do not give medicines other than those prescribed.

Projectile vomiting in a small baby is another dangerous sign, and should be reported at once. Spitting up, however, is quite normal and is merely the bringing up of milk during a feeding. Remember, though, that small children can become ill simply because of overindulgence, or because they get too excited. So consider all the relevant circumstances before you become anxious unnecessarily about your grandchild's condition.

Coping with problems

The birth of a grandchild may seem to herald a wonderful stage in life, but successful grandparenthood needs working at. No matter how stable a family situation is, problems inevitably arise from time to time, both of a practical and an emotional nature. As the senior member of the family, your grandchild's parents may turn to you for advice. But be careful because *uninvited* suggestions from in-laws can sometimes be seen as interference and, as such, may be rebuffed.

Taking an active interest in your grandchild's development will certainly mean that you, too, will be affected by any upsets that occur, because no family escapes the occasional quarrel. You may have to bite your tongue at times or turn the other cheek; but patience, a warm heart, and an understanding attitude will pay dividends in promoting healthy family relationships.

The working mother

One-parent families inevitably have more problems to cope with than most. Bringing up a child can be a lonely task for a single parent, and chores may seem endless at times if there is no one to share them. In such a situation, a grandparent may find he or she has an active role to play. But it is not only single mothers who have jobs outside the home. Whether or not to continue working is a crucial question facing today's new mother, one that would not have arisen twenty years ago other than in quite unusual circumstances and one that is currently the subject of much discussion. When there are no financial problems and a mother believes that the task of bringing up her children herself is an important one, no problems will arise. But the woman who has enjoyed a career may want to return to work soon after maternity leave and she will need to find suitable daycare or babysitting arrangements. This is often hard for a grandparent to understand, but a resentful mother is probably less beneficial to her child in the long run than is a happy working mother.

Studies have shown that it is important for an infant to be cared for by someone who not only looks after his physical needs but who will also play with him, talk to him, and cuddle him. A child needs this one-to-one relationship even at a very early stage. In times gone by, when the older generation often lived with the extended family, grandparents would have been on hand to take over as needed. But today, with families more separated geographically, professional daycare is called for. If, however, you live nearby and really want to care for your grandchild while his mother is at work, discuss the possibility with her because no mother wants to farm out her child to a stranger if she doesn't have to. Your daughter or daughter-in-law needs to have great confidence in you. You, in your turn, will need good reserves of energy and patience because it will not be that easy coping on a day-to-day basis with a small child after being away from this lifestyle for so long. But one thing is probable: there is likely to be far less risk of family jealousy for a child's affection if a grandparent looks after a toddler as a regular arrangement than if a babysitter or child-minder does so.

If arrangements are made for you to help out this way, it's better if you can look after your grandchild in his own familiar surroundings. Before too long, he will probably be attending a nursery school and you might be responsible for driving him there or for school-related activities. Consider all the ramifications before you offer to lend a hand in this way, and be sure to let everyone know at the first sign of finding the responsibility too much. Children can be very tiring, and it would be unwise from a health standpoint to extend yourself too greatly, however much you enjoy their company.

Hospitalization

If your grandchild ever has to go into the hospital, you will be concerned not only about his physical health and progress but about the effects on him of separation from the family. Some hospitals now allow mothers to stay with their infants or toddlers. But if rooming-in is not possible for some reason, you could perhaps share visiting times so that there is no chance that your grandchild will feel lonely. You could also help out by offering to look after any other sibling grandchildren. It is always a strenuous time for any family when someone is in the hospital and your practical assistance may be welcome. You can also be available in these ways if a parent is hospitalized, whether to have another baby, for observation, or for an operation. You might be able to stay at your grandchild's home, or to offer hospitality at your own house or apartment.

Never visit your grandchild in the hospital if you have a bad cold or infection, which could be caught by the young patient. When you visit, don't let your anxieties show. Your grandchild needs to feel confident in his new environment. Familiar playthings, books, or a new toy may help cheer him up. Jigsaw puzzles and felt-tip pens with plenty of paper are particularly suitable for a young patient. But don't expect to be greeted with the usual big hug. Your grandchild may be a little drowsy if he has had an anesthetic or he could be feeling upset because he is away from home. All this is quite normal Being hospitalized can be an unsettling experience for a small child; a great deal of sympathetic understanding is required. You may find he cries a little when you leave, but this is far better than slipping out unnoticed and letting your grandchild feel abandoned. Children in hospital need all the comfort you can possibly give them.

Preparing a child *in advance* for a possible hospital stay is wise, and one of the best ways you can do this is to explain what a hospital is whenever you pass one. Never use the prospect of being hospitalized as a threat. Unbelievable as it may seem, some parents (and grandparents) have been heard to do this when a child refuses to eat or continues to wet his bed at night, for instance.

There was a time when children were discouraged from visiting adults in the hospital. The thinking behind this was that they might pass on infections. It has now been established, however, that children are no more likely to pass on an infection than is an adult unless, of course, they have one of the common childhood diseases, in which case no sensible parent would let them visit a hospital anyway. So if by chance *you* find yourself in the hospital for some reason and would like your grandchild to visit, having checked first with a nurse and also with your grandchild's parents, you should find his visit will cheer you, in your turn.

Home nursing

The art of good home nursing lies in seeing that the young patient is as comfortable as possible, making allowances for loss of appetite while encouraging its return with light meals, and ensuring that the young patient does not lack company and amusement once on the mend. Make it as easy as possible for a child to take his medicine. Tablets can often be crushed into something palatable, and a reward may be called for in some instances. For a small baby, it may be necessary to give medicine by dropper. Have his head raised so that the drops are easily swallowed. Always check that you are giving medicine not only at the correct dosage but also at the intervals prescribed.

A matter of allergy

Some childhood conditions occur as an allergic reaction. Allergies sometimes run in families but they may take different forms: a reaction to a particular food, perhaps, or to household dust, feathers, hair, or fur. Children with celiac disease are allergic to wheat, and may need to be put on a gluten-free diet for the rest of their lives. Bear in mind any allergy your grandchild may have, if he or she comes to stay. You may, for instance have to provide a foam pillow rather than a feather one, or to take him or her to the ocean rather than to the countryside in August, if there is a hayfever problem. The asthma sufferer will also need special attention. Watch for signs of sudden breathlessness; it may have several causes. Keep your grandchild calm and relaxed, and call the doctor. If certain foods or items are contraindicated, don't feel that "just a little" won't hurt him; it will.

The handicapped child

It is simply a fact of life that not all children are within the range of 'normality'. Sometimes, quite out of the blue, a child is born with some form of physical or mental disability. Depending on the severity of the handicap, your support as a grandparent will be valued all the more if your grandchild is either born or becomes disabled. Once over the initial heartache, you may actually find that there is a very particular pleasure to be experienced from helping a handicapped child. Down's syndrome children, for example, are tremendously affectionate. Even if you have been told that your handicapped grandchild may never lead a full adult life, you can at least aim to provide all the love and security that will help him or her live as independently and happily as possible. Meeting with grandparents of similarly handicapped children should provide you with valuable encouragement as well as many practical ideas for helpful equipment and suitable outings and treats.

Language and behavior

At times, it can be very distressing to hear a young child using unpleasant language. Such vocabulary is often picked up at school and sometimes used at home out of sheer bravado. Make a fuss about it and your grandchild may try to annoy you again in this way, now that he knows his attention – seeking mechanism works. So the best approach is probably to ignore any 'bad' words he uses, or perhaps simply to tell him that you do not like the vocabulary he is using. You might also perhaps mention the matter to his parents.

Coping with problems

The Grandparent Game

How good a grandparent are you? Have you adapted well to the role? Follow the chart and assess the situations given. Similar problems sometimes arise even in the most idyllic family circles. A little forethought, however, will help you either avoid them altogether or cope with confidence.

1. You buy your grandson a puppy as a surprise for Christmas, without prior consultation with his parents. Move back to start.

2. Upset because your new granddaughter has not been given an old family name, you allow your displeasure to show. Move back three spaces.

3. You have a very bad cold, but still coo over the ten-day-old baby. Move back four spaces.

4. You forget that it is your five-year-old grandchild's birthday. Move back two spaces.

5. There is a disagreement between your grandchild's parents as to how he should be punished for stealing. You refuse to take sides. Move forward three spaces.

6. There is a bereavement in the family, which provides an excellent opportunity for you to talk with eight-year-old Daniel about the inevitability of growing old. Move forward three spaces.

7. Your son and daughter-in-law have just become divorced. When your grandchildren come to see you, you shower them with presents, as if to compensate for recent events. Move back two spaces.

8. You accept an invitation to attend an open house at your grandson's school. Move forward two spaces.

9. Before giving your grandchildren pocket money, you consult their parents. Move forward one space.

Coping with problems

10 Your grandchildren know that they only have to ask you for something and they will get it almost immediately. Move back two spaces.

11 Your larder and refrigerator always contain something suitable just in case the grandchilden stop by. Move forward one space.

12 You are delighted to look after your three-year-old grandchild while your daughter is in the hospital. Move forward one space.

13 Your son and daughter-in-law have decided to adopt a child. You give them every support in this. Move forward three spaces.

14 Following your daughter's recent marriage to a widower, you give a warm family welcome to your new stepgrandchild. Move forward two spaces.

15 You repeatedly reward your grandchild with sweets, even though his parents have asked you not to and you know that they are very bad for his teeth. Move back two spaces.

16 You always seem to telephone just when your daughter-in-law is fixing the children's supper. Move back one space.

17 You fail to tell your family about an inherited condition that runs in your side of the family. Move back four spaces.

18 You are jealous at times because your daughter-in-law's parents seem to see more of the grandchildren. You let your inner feelings fester. Move back three spaces.

19 You always embarrass your nine-year-old grandson by insisting he should hold your hand when you are out. Move back two spaces.

20 You secretly buy a crib for the new baby, and then are taken aback when you find your daughter and son-in-law have already bought one. Move back one space.

21 You repeatedly tell your daughter-in-law that "in our day we did things very differently". Move back two spaces.

79

Coping with problems

A matter of manners

Grandparents who were strict with their own children in the matter of good manners find it something of a surprise, if not a shock, to discover that their grandchildren are perhaps not so well schooled in this area. Certain aspects of good manners once considered very important are simply overlooked or totally disregarded today. It is rare to find a man, let alone a schoolboy, raising his hat when he meets a lady; children hardly ever offer their seats to an adult on a crowded bus, unless prompted to do so; the elderly and infirm are rarely invited to precede others. Twenty or thirty years ago, things were different.

Mutual respect is an essential part of living in a family unit, in a local community, and in society at large. Good manners, however, do not come naturally on the whole. Courtesy has to be taught, and the best way is by example and explanation. If you are looking after your grandchildren for the day and encounter a behavior problem, don't just lay down a rule but show why it is necessary.

Table manners do not come easily to small children. But practice makes perfect, so if you can experiment together, perhaps by giving a 'pretend' tea party, behavior is bound to improve. Children learn so much through play. But rehearsals will not be enough. By the time a child is three, he is old enough to sit with company for meals and to use the same china and silverware. Mealtimes are a social occasion, so if your grandchild wants to leave the table, have him ask for permission first.

Explain to your grandchild in a matter of fact way why we use words like 'please' and 'thank you', why people would like him to put his hand over his mouth when he yawns or coughs, or why he should use a handkerchief when he sneezes. If good manners are put in context with simple explanations, the chances are that he will both accept and adopt these niceties of behavior.

Problems can arise, however, if you make the mistake of criticizing and embarrassing your grandchild in public. You may not want him to interrupt while you are having a conversation; but if he forgets and butts in, instead of correcting him, try a simple, silent, but very effective reminder by putting your finger to your lips. When you have finished that particular part of the conversation, ask him what he had wanted.

Young children often find it difficult to take turns or to share. Toddlers commonly see their toys as an extension of themselves and are unwilling to let them go. This is, however, something they have to learn. One of the most successful ways of teaching it will be to keep your grandchild fully occupied while another child plays with his toy, or for him to swap toys for a few minutes and to see that they do come back to him. For a lesson in sharing, let one child cut a small cake in half and the other child choose which piece he would like. That way, both have role to play in the cake's division and fairness will prevail. Expose your grandchild to good manners and they should soon become second nature.

Family frictions

A child is bound to discover with time that, even in the most stable of families, adults have disagreements now and then. But avoid having actual shouting matches in front of a youngster. He or she may not yet be able to appreciate that arguments can sometimes be healthy and that people get over them.

But what if things go further? If parents find themselves unable to continue living together for whatever reason, what is a grandparent's role? For some grandparents, their child's divorce, and perhaps remarriage, will mean that they may see precious little of their grandchildren in the future. Approximately one in three marriages now ends in divorce, so these circumstances are by no means unusual. It can be a heartbreaking experience for grandparents. First and foremost, however, must come what is best for the child. Don't be shocked by the result of any proceedings, because today it is not always the mother who has custody of the children. Courts now go out of their way to determine which parent would provide the most beneficial influence.

If separation or divorce does occur, there is always a risk that a child may feel he is in some way to blame. If you sense he is having this reaction, do everything you can to reassure your grandchild that this is not the case. Explain that, although his parents may not be living together now, they have not divorced *him*.

Never grumble in his presence about his parents' behavior and encourage his parents not to do so either. The more normal everything can remain, the better, for family breakups of this kind can affect a child deeply. He may seem to cope well at home, with no marked change in behavior, but a profound reaction may sometimes show up elsewhere – in school, for example, where conduct may be disturbed.

Divorce doesn't have to be a harrowing experience for a child if it is handled sensibly. Most people would probably agree that it is far better for him or her in the long run than growing up in an atmosphere of tension. What a grandparent often finds something of a stumbling block, however, is the acceptance of a stepmother or stepfather taking over the parental role on a day-to-day basis, particularly if he or she is to be known as "daddy" or "mommy" (a confusing choice of name anyway in such circumstances).

Coping with problems

Perhaps the Cinderella story still lurks subconsciously in your mind. But a stepfather or stepmother will be having a difficult time, too; and for everyone involved there will be a tremendous amount of readjustment to be made. Take comfort in the thought that there is always great pressure on a second marriage to succeed – far greater, ironically, than there usually is on a first marriage. Grandparents should remember that the best parents and guardians for children are those who show them love, not necessarily those linked to them in purely biological terms.

Talking to strangers

Reading in the newspapers about the dreadful things that happen to children of all ages, we all wonder at times if something similar could occur in our own families and how we could best prevent it. At the same time, it is important not to turn the new generation into suspicious, distrusting individuals. How should you best explain to your grandchild, when he spends time with you, where the risks lie? How can you reinforce what his parents are teaching him?

Consistency is the key. Have a family discussion first so that you all agree on the same basic safety message. From the time he is very small, he should learn not to accept rides from strangers and always to tell his parents (or you, if you are looking after him) before going to another child's home or anywhere at all. But all this needs some further explanation, and it should be possible not to frighten a child unnecessarily but to tell him in a straightforward way that there are a few people in this world who are 'ill' and who may want to touch or harm him, which is why you do not want him to go wandering away without you. Of course, you should never leave a child on his own in a buggy outside a store, nor at home. In some countries, this is even illegal. Children should also be told never to open the door and let in a stranger, even if you are home.

Do's and dont's

Psychologists agree that the undisciplined child is likely to be a very confused one. Children definitely need guidelines in order to develop a sense of right and wrong. The problem for a grandparent, however, is what to do if some form of punishment seems necessary.

Your grandchild is probably on his best behavior when he is with you, but unfortunate situations do arise. There is not and never could be any 'ideal' form of punishment for every form of childhood misdemeanor.

Be consistent in your reactions. You may find it hard at times to resist giving a quick smack, but you might be able to achieve more simply by changing the tone of voice you use. An appeal to reason is usually a better first approach than a bribe. It may be years since you last had to reprimand a child but don't allow yourself to become overconcerned about it. All developing children need to feel that you *care,* and caring includes putting them on the right road as far as behavior is concerned.

Explaining about death

Most adults instinctively try to shield a child from knowing about death. It is certainly no easy business talking to a child about a bereavement but covering up is not a good idea either. What is most difficult for a child to understand is that death is irreversible, that a particular relative or his canary, cat, or puppy will not come back to life. That will take quite a bit of explaining. If it falls to you to do so, do not equate death with sleep. An explanation of that nature can induce night fears.

If someone in the family is seriously ill, you might gently warn the child that death might occur, explaining that the doctor is doing everything possible but that sometimes there is simply nothing more that can be done. Don't feel you need to hide your own grief either. Seeing this natural reaction and even attending the funeral should help your grandchild toward greater understanding of what has happened. Showing your grandchild how flowers bloom and fade and leaves bud and fall in seasonal cycles will also help him comprehend that human life also has a cycle. He will probably ask if *he* will die, too. You will have to confirm this, while reassuring him that it will not be for very many years, probably not until he is an extremely old person.

Small and large families

With today's lower birth rate, the only child is no longer a rarity. Traditionally thought of as spoiled and rather lonely, he will certainly need friends of his own age group, as will those who are virtually only children because of a large age gap. As a grandparent, you need to be careful not to overprotect him. You can also make sure that he gets to know any cousins because, for an only child, the extended family will be even more important. The child from a very large family, meanwhile, may have to bear more than his fair share of responsibilties, middle children may forever be landed with hand-me-down toys and clothes, and the youngest member of the family may be continually babied. Try to become as aware as you can of a grandchild's individual needs because of his position in the family. Your objectivity can help enormously in this respect.

A helping hand

"Born with a silver spoon in his mouth" says the old expression. Comparatively few of the world's children, however, are born into wealthy families and likely to receive a large inheritance from grandparents and parents alike, or any other relative or friend for that matter. Yet, whatever your financial status, it should be possible for you to pass on something to the new generation that will both serve as a remembrance and also be appreciated in its own right.

Custom dictates that the birth of a grandchild is celebrated with a gift of some kind. Sometimes this will be monetary: a deposit in a savings account, bonds of some kind, shares, stock, or a silver ingot perhaps. But the token with which you choose to make the baby's debut doesn't have to be financial. Resources may not extend to this or, quite simply, you may prefer to give something rather more original in concept. A hand-embroidered sampler, with specific wording, is bound to be treasured. A bible or prayer book with a personalized message can be passed on for generations. A case of wine could be put away, to be drunk when fully matured in celebration of your grandchild reaching his age of majority.

Items for a layette or the nursery will also be welcome. In fact, there are numerous possibilities. But whatever you choose, the chances are you can expect to have more grandchildren over the next few years whose births you will want also to celebrate. Any helping hand you give might have to span more than one new infant, so you may want to budget carefully. Favoritism is something to be avoided at all costs.

Where there's a will

Many grandparents choose to take out an insurance policy of some kind and to alter their wills on the birth of a grandchild. This is something about which you should definitely seek expert, individual opinion by consulting your legal advisor or accountant, not only to ensure that the document is a legal and binding one but also in order to consider the best way in which you can make provision for your grandchild's future, since the legal and tax implications will vary from situation to situation. You may want to establish a trust of some kind, perhaps making a stipulation that any legacy should remain untouched by your grandchild until he or she reaches a certain age. Check carefully on the legalities of this.

Make specific mention in a will of any objects (a stamp or coin collection, perhaps, or a painting) that you would like one particular grandchild to receive. Many people are far happier to receive an heirloom of some kind (no matter what its intrinsic value) than to be left money by their grandparents; for if your relationship has been a good one, they will wish to have some object that you, in your time, greatly prized. The granddaughter who has always enjoyed your cooking may be thrilled to receive your collection of well-loved recipes; a grandson may be delighted with some item of furniture that once graced your home; another grandchild might appreciate a stamp or coin collection, or some of your books.

Nostalgia runs deep. Don't underestimate today's possessions either. Even the seemingly ordinary household objects of today are the antiques of tomorrow. The ethical will of old – in which parents and grandparents left pearls of wisdom for the next generation in addition to or in place of money or objects – is yet another variation on the theme.

Making allowances

There are many other ways in which you can lend a helping hand financially during your lifetime, even if this has to be rather limited. You may want to give your grandchildren pocket money from time to time but you really should consult first with their parents. In general, however, it's better for you, as a grandparent rather than a parent, to give pocket money on an irregular basis, so that they do not come to expect it from you. Very small children are also generally happier with several coins of low value than a larger coin or note of the same value; quite understandably, in their eyes, several coins seem to be worth more.

You may also want to discuss with their parents the idea of rewarding your grandchildren for odd jobs that they do for you – cutting the grass, polishing the car, or tidying up, for instance. They will probably enjoy earning some pocket money.

Encourage them to learn the art of saving, perhaps by opening an account of some kind that will accrue interest – again, with their parents' agreement. In this respect, inform yourself of the tax aspects of the saving account both for you and for your grandchild. A money box makes a good present, too, as does a purse.

Other ways in which grandparents are

A helping hand

If you would like to give your grandchild pocket money from time to time, remember to consult his or her parents first, and do your best to ensure it is used wisely. There are of course many other ways you can help to give the new generation a good start in life. But perhaps the most valuable contribution you could make is not one of a financial nature but the care and attention of a loving grandparent.

sometimes able to assist incude the provision of music lessons, perhaps personally if they have skills in this area, or by paying for them on a regular basis. However, private tuition of this kind does not come cheaply these days. The more financially secure grandparents may be able to offer to contribute school tuition, perhaps by taking out some form of education policy soon after the birth of a grandchild. But even if you are able to do this, you need to ensure that a private education is indeed something that the parents believe is right and thus a possible option. The decision about the type of education your grandchild is to receive is, in the final analysis, quite rightly theirs. Once again, you need to check on the tax implications.

Unusual gifts

Grandparents' gifts can, of course, take still other forms and, again, don't have to be costly, and may even at times be free. If, for instance, you are planning a holiday abroad, you may find that some travel companies offer accommodation without cost for children under a certain age, as long as they share a room with you. For an older grandchild, meanwhile, you might consider paying for driving lessons, clothing, a set of encyclopedias or college text books, the tools of his trade if he is taking up a practical career, perhaps a home computer, or even items of furniture for an apartment if you are in the financial position to provide such things.

As far as any lifetime financial gifts are concerned, you should consult a professional in order to take advantage of local fiscal laws. There may be ways, too, in which you can make a secret gift to your grandchild.

Such provisions are a bonus for any grandchild but they are by no means everything. Indeed, perhaps the most valuable helping hand of all is a caring presence. For nothing in the way of riches can possibly replace the good start in life that a warm extended family circle can provide for the growing child.

It could be, too, that your grandchildren, as they grow into adulthood, will welcome the opportunity to assist *you* in a number of ways. Beware the temptation to be too independent! As you will find, there is a great joy to be had in lending a helping hand to another generation in the family.

Family photographs

Like most grandparents, you probably often proudly show snapshots of the new generation to friends and extended family. Perhaps you are even a crack photographer yourself, and produce some excellent results. For many people, the birth of a grandchild will mean a rekindled interest in photography, particularly portraiture, and perhaps the purchase of new camera.

What sort of equipment will be most useful? There are so many cameras on the market that, at first, the choice can be overwhelming. If simplicity is the key and you have not handled a camera much in the past, you'll do best with a disc camera. This will probably have an automatic film advance, automatic exposure, and automatic flash. A disc camera is easy to load and to carry around, and small enough to fit into a handbag or pocket, but you may find that the special film required is a little more expensive than the film you have been used to buying.

Transparencies or prints?

Before you buy a new camera, make up your mind whether you will always only want color prints, or whether you might like to have color transparencies sometimes, or to shoot in black and white. Compact 35mm cameras, which will produce all three, are especially suitable for photographing children. Some cameras come with automatic focus and exposure and will warn you if there is too little light and if a flash is necessary. With a manual camera, you need to set apertures and shutter speeds.

Pictures with a difference

For the impatient – and, of course, for family parties – an instant camera (like a Polaroid) can be tremendous fun. It will only be a couple of minutes before you have the result in your hand, but the image is unlikely to be as successful as the one you'll get with a standard camera. The film is also likely to be quite expensive but, then, it does include processing. You can also use an instant camera to check on the compositional apsects of a family group shot. Although 3-D cameras are also now available and the resulting prints are quite effective, there are limitations on size, and the process is still fairly expensive.

Once you have mastered the basic techniques, practice, and more practice, will help you produce better results. Don't expect to become an expert overnight. Even the top professionals reject a lot of their own work and it often takes several rolls of film to achieve that one very special shot that will be treasured.

To help you take the best possible pictures of your grandchildren, we have asked several photographers to offer you some of their own professional secrets. A good photography manual will be a useful tool for technical reference, but only by making a few mistakes on the way will your technique improve.

Choose backgrounds for your pictures that are as uncluttered as possible so that the subject does not lose prominence. Get your grandchild to wear something bright, if you are shooting in color, and choose a plain background if he has on a patterned sweater or shirt. Your pictures will be more successful from the point of view of composition if your subject is slightly off center. For a group portrait, remember to place the tallest in the family at the back, with the others sitting or kneeling, and try to get everyone looking towards the camera. They don't need to be actually saying "cheese", but it will certainly make for a more lively image if you encourage all your subjects to smile. When shooting outdoors, check that harsh sunight is not causing squinting; this looks unattractive in a photograph. The best photographs are not always taken at home; parks, beaches, and adventure playgrounds make excellent locations.

Watch out for strange effects! By checking carefully in the viewfinder, you should be able to ensure that a lamp or tree, for example, is not positioned so that it appears to be growing out of the subject's head! Check on distance, too. Your main subject should, as a rule, not be more than nine feet or so away for a successful portrait. He will otherwise tend to get lost in the picture, and the exposure will be wasted.

Using props to good effect

Consider the framing of your subjects, too. Objects like a decorative chair or an archway can contribute a great deal. Favorite toys or pets can also make excellent props, adding points of interest to an otherwise straightforward portrait. Show your older grandchild with a musical instrument he is learning. Use rattles to attract a younger child's attention.

Family photographs

Children are by nature rather impatient, so you always need to work quickly. When taking a picture of a baby, the trick is not to make the infant appear too insignificant in the final image. Get in close, but instead of looking down at your grandchild, get down to floor or crib level. Try photographing your new grandchild with his parents, too, in order to achieve a sense of scale, as well as contrast in size and strength. A tiny frail baby, cradled against a hairy chest, makes a very appealing picture. Small babies are usually happiest with nothing on, so that they are free to move about, so you may want to photograph your new grandchild nude, providing the room is warm. The best background for this sort of picture is a neutral shade of cream, particularly for dark-skinned babies, or a deep shade. A baby can also be propped up with cushions from about the age of eight weeks to provide a satisfactory pose.

A pictorial record

Why not start a complete pictorial record of your grandchild's development? You can start from day one, when you visit your daughter or daughter-in-law and the newborn baby in the hospital. Try to get a number of shots of the baby being fed, bathed, and dressed, as well as when he is soundly asleep and when he cries. Keep your camera handy, with film loaded, just in case something rather special happens that demands an immediate picture. Keep shooting and don't stint on film if you really want to achieve good results. Show him crawling, standing, and walking. See, too, that you have a pictorial record of habits like thumb-sucking or twirling hair. Cover memorable moments, as well: the first tricycle, or a birthday party. A shot of a baby catching sight of himself in a mirror is also very effective.

The candid camera

The best photographs of small children are those that are natural and relaxed. Watch for typical expressions. It's always worthwhile capturing them on film because it is only too easy to forget what children looked like at a certain age if you do not have these reminders. Try to get your grandchildren used to the camera, perhaps by showing them how it operates, and show them your results.

Once they are used to the camera, you can snap away without them being too aware of what you are doing. Photographs of them dressing up, having fun on a jungle gym, or building with bricks will be delightful images to have, as will candid shots featuring chocolate-coated mouths, paint-stained hands, muddy boots and crumpled clothes. You may want to take the occasional formal portrait, for which you might like him to get spruced up, but it will be far more realistic to show him not as Little Lord Fauntleroy but as a busy, growing, lively child.

Avoiding common faults

If your pictures turn out to be too dark, you need to ask yourself first of all whether there was sufficient light and, secondly, whether the subject was too distant. Poor color could be due to dismal weather conditions or to the processing. If the horizontals are not straight, you may not have been holding the camera steady. If the pictures are not sharp, perhaps you need to hold the camera more firmly. Check on the focus next time. It may help to consider whether you have better results when taking photographs if you wear your glasses or if you remove them. If your subject always appears too close to the edge of the frame, you may need to look more carefully in the viewfinder on the next occasion.

A camera for your grandchild

Children are often enthusiastic about taking photographs themselves, so you may consider either handing on your own camera or buying your grandchild a new one for a birthday or for Christmas. Get professional advice on a model that is suitable for a child of his or her age. It should be quite solid and not easily broken if dropped by accident. If you aren't going to be the one constantly providing film, check first with his parents that they are prepared to supply film on a regular basis because photography can be an expensive hobby if carried out enthusiastically. The young photographer must have film with which to practice. Ask to see his work, and encourage him to experiment with different subject matter and techniques.

Using a camera can provide an enormous amount of pleasure. But after you have either printed the film yourself or had it processed, then what? Some of your images will almost certainly be of merit, while others will be of great sentimental value to you personally, no matter how technically imperfect. You will undoubtedly get even more enjoyment from your photography if you consider some of the many ways in which photographs can be creatively displayed. You will also need carefully to consider the sort of film you require, negative or transparency, for the type of prints you would finally like to have. Seek professional advice, if in doubt, before you begin shooting. Movie photography, which requires a different approach, will provide equally exciting opportunities for recording your grandchild's development.

Family photographs

The family album

If you have a collection of family photographs but have not yet put them into an album, or would like to rearrange those you have, consider organizing them without delay. Like all proud grandparents, you will doubtless want to add photographs featuring the new generation and if you wish to place the pictures sequentially, you first need to have put in order your pictorial record of the family's history.

Many people have old family pictures tucked away in boxes, bringing them out only occasionally, but it really is a shame not to display them to good effect. As they grow, your grandchildren will love to see photographs of their parents when small, and of the extended family, too. If you have some prints that have faded or become stained, consider having them saved by a professional restorer. If you have good photographic skills, you may even be able to do this yourself, with the aid of a technical manual. Consider having some reprinted, too, in sepia.

There are now many albums on the market, in a variety of shapes and sizes. Compiling a book of family images doesn't have to be just a matter of fixing snapshots with corner hinges. Arrange your pictures in interesting groupings, changing the pace so that some pages will be packed, while others feature a single image. See that all your photographs are captioned with as much information as possible, incuding dates, names, location and relevant or irreverent comment, perhaps, to accompany humorous shots. You might make your own looseleaf album, using colored card pages fastened within a binder, or look around for a antique album. It might need a bit of repair but will possibly make a suitably nostalgic setting for your family pictures. You will only be able to trace the family in this way back to the mid-nineteenth century, when photography was first developed; but even so, in turning the album's pages with you, your grandchild will come face to face with some fascinating social history. Changing fashions and hairstyles, old school and army uniforms, houses and furniture: all will provide delightful clues to the family's way of life over the last hundred years or so. Watching for interesting family likenesses can provide enormous fun for you all, too.

Displaying family portraits

Some old family portraits and groups – and some new ones, too – are so appealing that you may want to have them on permanent display. There are many ways in which you can do this: perhaps on a tabletop, on a piano or sideboard, on a mantlepiece, on the wall, as a miniature within a locket or on a keychain, for instance.

If you have old family photographs, such as those shown here, bring them out occasionally to show to your grandchildren. They are bound to enjoy seeing what you were like as a child, and family likenesses are fun for everyone to spot. Changes in fashion and hairstyles make for a fascinating lesson in social history, too, you will find.

Family photographs

You may choose to arrange a grouping of portraits on a small table or shelf, in a variety of frames, perhaps placing portraits of your grandchildren next to earlier family pictures. Transparent cubes provide an interesting way of displaying several portraits at once or, for a wall display, you can group several portraits together within the same mat and frame. For a more informal display, you can have recent family snapshots mounted on a board. You might consider, too, having a whole wall of family portraits. It is not difficult to have prints especially made to fit an available space. Favorite pictures can even be made into poster-type prints, if this type of presentation is more suited to your decor. You can also select a variety of finishes – glossy or pearl, for example – or request an enlargement of part of a picture, if there is sufficient detail. Sepia toning, vignetting, and hand-coloring are old crafts that some studios still practice today, and that may also lend themselves to certain contemporary pictures.

Lighting has an important contribution to make to a successful display. You can spotlight a portrait dramatically or try for a more subdued effect. Both very strong sunlight and intense artificial light can, however, over a period of time, cause certain color prints to fade. So do position your family portraits very carefully. Only by experimenting will you finally achieve a really effective arrangement.

Creative framing

Leather, velvet, wood and metal frames can all display a portrait to great advantage. But it is also fun to make decorative frames yourself. Spare fabric can be used to cover an ordinary cardboard frame, and it can be particularly effective if it coordinates with other soft furnishings in a room. Shells, too, perhaps gathered on a family holiday, can be used to make an attractive frame. Keep an eye open for old picture and mirror frames, which can be used to enhance photography. You may come across a ghastly painting, for instance, in a rather grand frame, and buy it for the frame alone. Consider carefully the sort of mat you choose for your photographs. The shade, shape and size of mat can completely change the mood of a picture, emphasizing different qualities. Double and triple mats can create particularly interesting effects. You can use decorative pages from old albums as mats, too. Sometimes, however, you may prefer to hang a really striking picture without a frame, mounting it on wood or hardboard, or simply between clips and glass. The range of effects you can achieve by careful choice of frame is infinite.

Original applications

Photography is an extremely versatile medium, and its images need not be confined to paper alone. Plates, window blinds, cushions and screens can all be decorated with photographic portraiture. By looking at your family pictures in a creative way, you can probably come up with a wealth of alternative applications for the images you love.

Photo Linen is coated with photographic emulsion, and can be used in many exciting ways, but in black and white only. You can feature a portrait of your grandchild on a wallhanging or table covering, for instance. If you do your own photographic printing, you should not find the process very complicated, or you may find a commercial laboratory willing to transfer an image to Photo Linen for you. Printing on china, wood, glass, canvas, and leather can also be quite successful with the use of special emulsion. Seek out a good guide to such printing techniques. Personalized placemats, bibs, toy boxes and even lunch boxes can all be embellished with photographs of various members of your family. Possibilities are endless, with plenty of scope for creating pictorial heirlooms that all the family are bound to treasure.

The family tree

Deeply ingrained in us all is a need, although perhaps an unconscious one, to 'belong'. For many of us, this need applies not only to a contemporary family circle but also to the past. Anecdotes about our parents as children, and our grandparents, too, make for fascinating listening. Only too often, however, families are left without any written record at all of names, dates, marriages or offspring, so that many do not know the maiden name of a grandmother or great-aunt, for instance, or at what point an unusual or foreign surname came into the family line, or even after whom they may be named. How wonderful, then, to create a family tree!

There are professional organizations and societies that will research family origins, but the cost could be prohibitive, and the work involved very complex, if not impossible, when family ties extend to other continents, where until recently community records may have been sparse if not nonexistant.

There could be no finer gift to pass on to your grandchildren than a family tree, as detailed as you can make it. The problem lies in compiling the information. Starting points might be an old family bible (with entries about specific family events), wedding invitations, birth announcement cards, and certificates of various kinds which may have been kept. Contact other member of the family who could help you fill in any gaps in the tree as you compile it. There are various specialist genealogical libraries, too, which may prove helpful in assisting you to track down details about previous generations.

You have probably seen examples of tables that show lineage and dates in history books. The most straightforward way of drawing up a tree is to make one for your own line and one for your spouse's. This keeps the final diagram from becoming unnecessarily complicated. Sketch the trees in pencil first, to avoid making unnecessary mistakes on the final drafts, for which pages are provided in this chapter.

In one example given, you will see that all those of the same generation are shown on the same level, with straight bar lines linking parents and children. We have omitted details of brothers and sisters, aunts and uncles, first and second cousins and so on, for clarity's sake, but you could create a tree with as much detail as you can trace. Another

In this style of family tree, headings are used to identify the various generations.

A family tree can also be drawn using a circular format. Your own name features centrally.

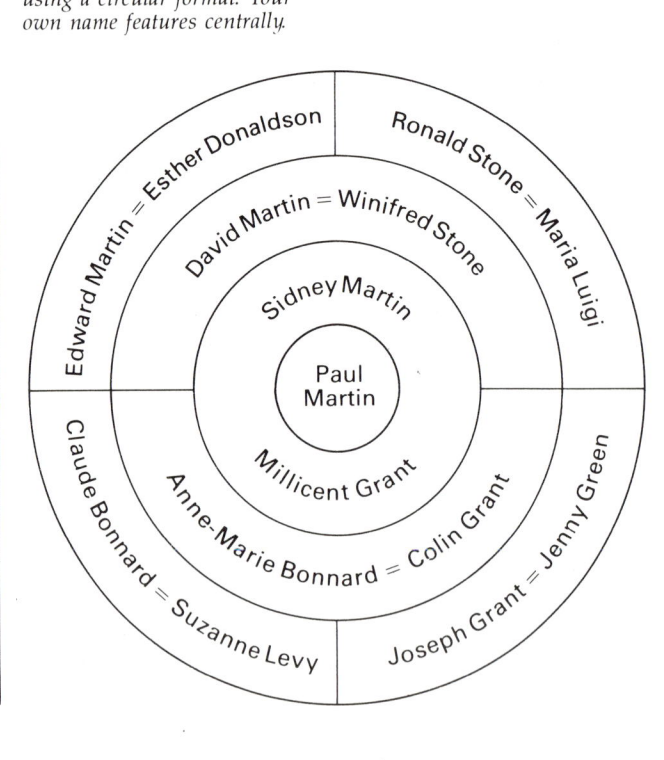

Parents	Grandparents	Great-grandparents	Great-great-grandparents
Rosemary Collins	Anne Murray	Sarah Temple	Rachael Smithson
			Charles Temple
		Daniel Murray	Barnaby Murray
			Clara Clarke
	Ralph Collins	John Collins	Florence Gardiner
			Oscar Collins
		Clara Brown	Samuel Brown
			Gertrude Crisp
Paul Martin	Millicent Grant	Anne-Marie Bonnard	Suzanne Levy
			Claude Bonnard
		Colin Grant	Joseph Grant
			Jenny Green
	Sidney Martin	David Martin	Edward Martin
			Esther Donaldson
		Winifred Stone	Ronald Stone
			Maria Luigi

The family tree

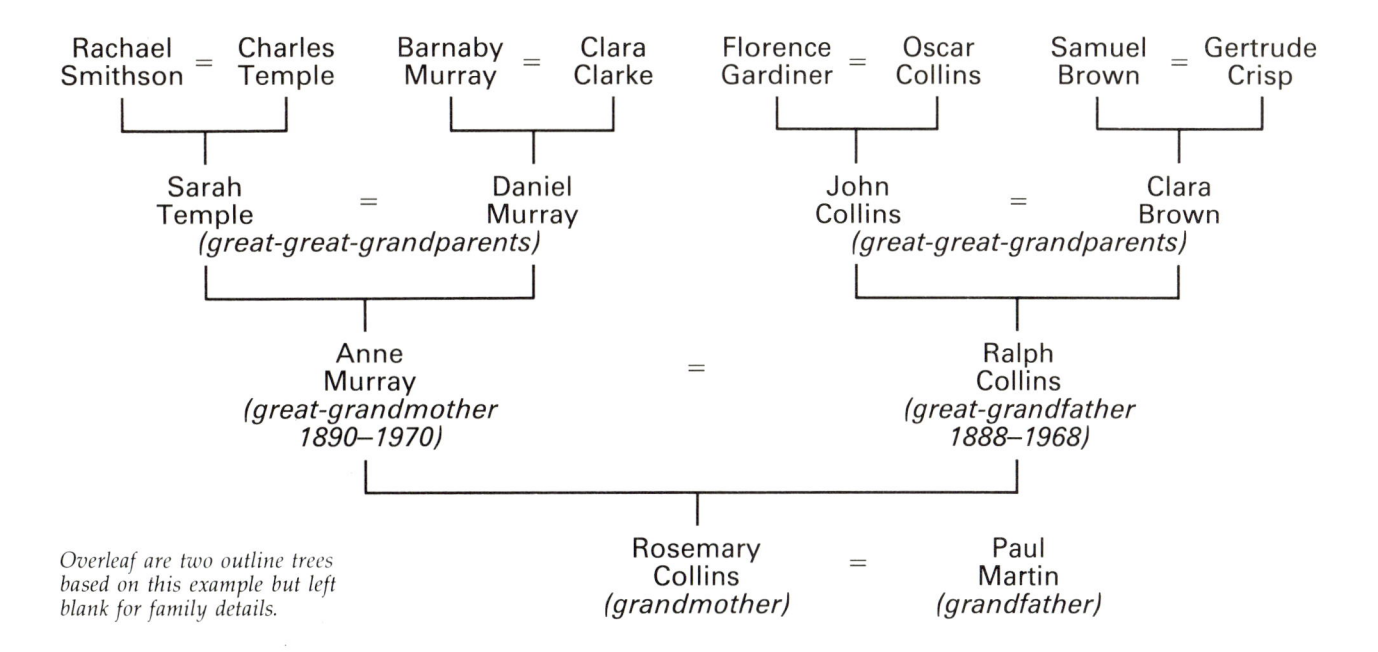

```
Rachael    = Charles     Barnaby   = Clara        Florence   = Oscar       Samuel    = Gertrude
Smithson     Temple      Murray      Clarke       Gardiner     Collins     Brown       Crisp
     |_____|              |_____|               |_____|             |_____|
           |                       |                        |                       |
         Sarah         =        Daniel                    John         =         Clara
         Temple                 Murray                    Collins                Brown
                  (great-great-grandparents)                       (great-great-grandparents)
                        |_____|                               |_____|
                                |                                              |
                              Anne                         =                 Ralph
                              Murray                                         Collins
                        (great-grandmother                             (great-grandfather
                           1890–1970)                                      1888–1968)
                                            |_____|
                                                    |
                                                Rosemary        =        Paul
                                                Collins                  Martin
                                              (grandmother)           (grandfather)
```

Overleaf are two outline trees based on this example but left blank for family details.

example illustrated starts with a central circle in which your own name is written. This is then extended, with a further circle featuring the next generation back. Dates can be added under the names. Simply leave a particular segment blank if you cannot find the relevant name. One disadvantage of this method, however, is that no space can be left for your children and grandchildren to continue the tree. A new circular tree must be drawn to incorporate each new generation. Nor is there room to feature siblings and relatives other than those in the direct line. A third example is shown as a simple table, headed with titles that immediately distinguish the generations.

All families have some sort of skeleton in the closet, so don't be too perturbed if your family tree reveals information that is surprising or even startling. Other discoveries may include fascinating family names (which forthcoming generations may choose to adopt) and interesting links with particular families. In this way, you will become a genealogist in your own right. Surnames can give clues to a forebear's trade (Baker, Butler or Goldsmith, for instance), appearance (Schwartzbart – that is, 'black beard' in German – and Grand are examples), or descendency (Peterson – son of Peter). You may also find a change of surname. An ancestor may have emigrated and chosen a new name that would be more easily pronounced or that would disguise an origin, a change from Horowicz to Horn or from Van der Veld to Vine, for example.

When recording information, full names, however long, should always be included. You may also want to keep an annotated book with entries about those featured in the tree, including details about their professions, addresses and appearances if known.

Your grandchild will probably also find it interesting to collect anecdotes about the schools you attended and your favorite subjects, the sort of clothes you wore when young, the games you played, your toys, special family occasions and your war recollections, perhaps. All such information can provide fascinating additional background to the family tree, and may perhaps be collated in a special note book.

You might encourage your grandchild, too, to investigate other people who would feature in the drawn-up family tree if there was sufficient room: his grandfather's brothers and sisters, for instance. Explain the terminology given to such family relationships. Your grandchildren's parents' cousins are his first cousins once removed, and their children are his second cousins. Children of first cousins are second cousins to one another: so that the children of your grandchild's first cousins will be second cousins to his as-yet-unborn children, and first cousins once removed to him. The convention is that, if cousins are not on the same level of descent, they are known as first, second and even third cousins once removed. It may take a little time to master this at first: but once the basic principle has been grasped, working out the intricacies of family relationships can be a fascinating task.

The two pages that follow have been tabulated specifically for you to draw up your own family tree. Make copies to present to other members of your family. A very decorative tree could be framed for display. Appoint yourself the family historian and create a memento that all your relatives will value greatly.

The family tree

Grandmother's family

The family tree

Grandfather's family

Memorandum

The pages that follow have been left blank for you to keep notes as reminders about birthdays, school holiday dates, special food likes and dislikes, emergency telephone numbers, and any other details relevant to a grandchild's welfare. You will also find space for keeping a record about outings and treats, as well as gifts, so that you won't double up on these by mistake. If you have more grandchildren, insert additional loose-leaf pages into *The Grandparents' Handbook.*

Grandchild's full name
Date of birth

Emergency telephone numbers   *Parents' work places*
Doctor
Hospital   *Other relatives*

Diet: special likes and dislikes, allergies, etc.

School

Hobbies and interests

Outings and dates

Gifts

Additional notes

Memorandum

Grandchild's full name
Date of birth

Emergency telephone numbers
Doctor
Hospital

Parents' work places

Other relatives

Diet: special likes and dislikes, allergies, etc.

School

Hobbies and interests

Outings and dates

Gifts

Additional notes

Memorandum

Grandchild's full name
Date of birth

Emergency telephone numbers
Doctor
Hospital

Parents' work places

Other relatives

Diet: special likes and dislikes, allergies, etc.

School

Hobbies and interests

Outings and dates

Gifts

Additional notes

Memorandum

Grandchild's full name
Date of birth

Emergency telephone numbers
Doctor
Hospital

Parents' work places

Other relatives

Diet: special likes and dislikes, allergies, etc.

School

Hobbies and interests

Outings and dates

Gifts

Additional notes

Index

Accidents
    emergency treatment 72-73
    prevention of 25, 26-29
Adoption 16
Age, average, of grandparents 7
Air, travel by 31-32
Allergies 77
Allowances 82-83

Baths 14, 22
Beach, day at the 37
Bed, having baby in 10
Bed-wetting 22
Bedtime, *see* Sleep
Bereavement 35, 81
Birthdays, *see* Gifts
Books 69, 70
Bottle-feeding 9, 13, 21 31
Breakfast, *see* Recipes
Breast-feeding 9

Car, travel by 31, 32
Carrying the baby 8, 12, 30
Childbirth 8, 9
Circumcision 9
Circus 36
Clothing, for baby
    see Layette
Colic 10
    see also Crying
Cooking, for grandchildren 20-21
    see also Recipes
Countryside 37
Crying 9, 23

Dangers, at home 25-29
    outside the home 30-33
Death, *see* Bereavement
Desserts, *see* Recipes
Diapers, changing of 12-13, 22
Diet, *see* Food, Recipes
Dinner, *see* Recipes
Discipline 81
Diseases, hereditary 7-8
Divorce 80-81
Doctor, when to call 72-75
Dreams 22
Drinks, *see* Recipes

Eating out 30-31
Emergencies 72-73

Family size 81
Family tree 88-91
Father's role 8
Favoritism 16-17
Feeding 13, 20, 21
    see also Bottle feeding, Breast feeding, food, Recipes
Financial advice 82-83
First Aid 72-73
Food 30, 33
    see also Recipes

Games 60-65
Gardening 38-41
Genetic counseling 8
Gifts, ideas for 10-12, 66-71, 82-83, 85
Growth, rate of 14-15

Handicap 8, 77
Heredity 7, 8
Holidays 32-33
Hospitalization 76-77

Illness 25, 74-77
Insurance 33

Language, *see* Speech

Layette 10-12
Lifting the baby 8, 12
Lunch, *see* Recipes

Manners 80
Memorandum 92-95
Museums 36

Natural childbirth 9
Nursery equipment 12
    see also Layette

Outings 30-33, 36-37
    see also Treats

Pacifiers 9
Pets 34-35
Photography, family 84-87
Pillows 12, 20
Play, *see* Toys
Poisoning, *see* First Aid
Pocket money 82-83
    see also Allowances
Post-natal
    check-up 10
    depression 10
    exercises 10
Presents, *see* Gifts
Problems, family 18, 76-81

Quarrels, family 80-81

Recipes 52-59
Routine 23
Rules 25, 81

Safety, in the home 20, 25, 26-29, 68
    outside the home 30-33, 37
    see also First Aid
Sea, travel by 32
Separation 80-81
Shopping 30
Sleeping arrangements 20, 22
    problems 22, 23
Smoking 10
Snacks 21, 30, 31
    see also Recipes
Speech 23, 77
Spoiling 16-17
Sports 37
Step-grandchildren 16
Strangers, talking to 81
Sunburn 33
Supper, *see* Recipes

Television 24
Temper tantrums 25
Toys 66-71
    to make 42-51
Train, travel by 32
Traveling 30-33
Treats 36-37
    see also Outings
Twins 24

Vegetables, *see* Recipes
Visits, from grandchildren 20-25

Will, making of 82
Wind 10
Work, mother's return to 76

Yard, activities in 38-41
    see also Gardening

Zoo 36

Further Reading

A Book For Grandmothers
Ruth Goode (McGraw-Hill, 1976)

The Taming of the C.A.N.D.Y. Monster by Vicki Lansky (Meadowbrook, 1978)

Emergency Baby First Aid
by Clifford Rubin
(Berkley, 1979)

Self-Esteem: A Family Affair
by Jean Illsley Clarke
(Winston Press, 1978)

Parent Awareness
by Saf Lerman (Winston Press, 1980)

The Family Doctor's Health Tips
by Keith Sehnert
(Meadowbrook, 1981)

The Parents' Guide to Baby and Child Medical Care Ed: Terril Hart (Meadowbrook, 1982)

Sweet Dreams for Little Ones
by Michael Pappas (Winston Press, 1982)

What to Do When There's Nothing to Do Ed: Elizabeth Gregg (Avon, 1982)

Practical Parenting Tips
Ed: Vicki Lansky
(Meadowbrook, 1982)

The Grandparenting Book
by Norman Bowman et al
(Blossom Valley, 1982)

Raising Brothers and Sisters Without Raising the Roof
by Carole and Andrew Calladine (Winston Press, 1983)

The Baby Massage Book
by Tina Heinl (Prentice-Hall, 1983)